A Guide to Stellar Reviews: Crafting Effective Responses

While every precaution has been taken in the preparation of this book, the publisher assumes no responsibility for errors or omissions, or for damages resulting from the use of the information contained herein.

A GUIDE TO STELLAR REVIEWS: CRAFTING EFFECTIVE RESPONSES

First edition. January 19, 2024.

ISBN: 979-8224622733

Written by DIgital Commerce Girl.

---

1. https://booksbyai.app/bBrA6NiTkbJBDKrb/2.2

2. https://booksbyai.app/bBrA6NiTkbJBDKrb/2.2

1 Understanding the Importance of Stellar Reviews

1.1 The Power of Positive Reviews

Positive reviews have the power to significantly impact a business's success. In today's digital age, online reviews have become a crucial part of the consumer decision-making process. When potential customers are considering purchasing a product or service, they often turn to online reviews to gather information and gauge the experiences of others. Positive reviews can serve as powerful endorsements, influencing potential customers to choose your business over competitors.

1.1.1 Building Trust and Credibility

Positive reviews help build trust and credibility for your business. When customers see that others have had positive experiences with your products or services, it instills confidence in your brand. Positive reviews act as social proof, assuring potential customers that they can trust your business to deliver on its promises.

1.1.2 Increasing Sales and Revenue

Positive reviews can directly impact your bottom line by increasing sales and revenue. When potential customers read positive reviews, they are more likely to convert into paying customers. According to a study by BrightLocal, 88% of consumers trust online reviews as much as personal recommendations. Positive reviews can be the deciding factor that pushes a potential customer to make a purchase.

1.1.3 Improving Search Engine Rankings

Positive reviews also play a role in improving your business's visibility in search engine rankings. Search engines like Google take into account the quantity and quality of reviews when determining the relevance and credibility of a business. Businesses with a higher number of positive reviews are more likely to appear higher in search results, increasing their online visibility and attracting more potential customers.

1.1.4 Enhancing Brand Reputation

Positive reviews contribute to enhancing your brand's reputation. When customers leave positive reviews, they are essentially endorsing your business and recommending it to others. This positive word-of-mouth can have a significant impact on your brand's reputation, both online and offline. A strong brand reputation can attract new customers, retain existing ones, and differentiate your business from competitors.

1.1.5 Encouraging Customer Loyalty

Positive reviews can foster customer loyalty and repeat business. When customers have a positive experience and leave a glowing review, they are more likely to become loyal advocates for your brand. These loyal customers are not only more likely to continue purchasing from your business but also more likely to recommend your products or services to their friends, family, and social networks.

1.1.6 Leveraging Positive Reviews for Marketing

Positive reviews can be powerful marketing tools. You can leverage these reviews in your marketing materials, such as on your website, social media platforms, and in advertising campaigns. Sharing positive reviews with your audience helps to reinforce the positive image of your brand and can attract new customers who are influenced by the experiences of others.

1.1.7 Engaging with Customers

Responding to positive reviews provides an opportunity to engage with your customers and show appreciation for their support. By taking the time to respond to positive reviews, you demonstrate that you value your customers' feedback and are committed to providing excellent customer service. This engagement can further strengthen the relationship between your business and its customers.

1.1.8 Encouraging More Positive Reviews

Responding to positive reviews can also encourage more customers to leave positive feedback. When customers see that you actively engage with and appreciate positive reviews, they are more likely to share their own positive experiences. This cycle of positive reviews can create a virtuous circle, further enhancing your business's reputation and attracting more customers.

In summary, positive reviews have the power to build trust, increase sales, improve search engine rankings, enhance brand reputation, foster customer loyalty, and serve as effective marketing tools. By understanding the importance of positive reviews and crafting effective responses, you can harness the power of positive feedback to propel your business towards success.

1.2 The Impact of Reviews on Business Success

Online reviews have become an integral part of the consumer decision-making process. In today's digital age, potential customers rely heavily on reviews to determine the quality and credibility of a business. As a result, the impact of reviews on business success cannot be underestimated.

1.2.1 Building Trust and Credibility

Positive reviews play a crucial role in building trust and credibility for your business. When potential customers see a high number of positive reviews, it instills confidence in them that your products or services are of high quality and reliable. Positive reviews act as social proof, assuring potential customers that others have had a positive experience with your business.

Furthermore, positive reviews can help establish your business as an authority in your industry. When customers consistently leave positive reviews, it demonstrates that your business is knowledgeable, trustworthy, and capable of delivering exceptional products or services.

1.2.2 Increasing Sales and Revenue

Reviews have a direct impact on sales and revenue. Numerous studies have shown that businesses with positive reviews experience higher conversion rates and increased sales. When potential customers read positive reviews, they are more likely to make a purchase or engage with your business.

Positive reviews also have the power to attract new customers. When satisfied customers share their positive experiences, it can generate word-of-mouth referrals and recommendations. This organic form of marketing can lead to a steady stream of new customers, ultimately boosting your sales and revenue.

1.2.3 Improving Search Engine Rankings

Online reviews can significantly impact your business's visibility in search engine results. Search engines, such as Google, take into account the quantity and quality of reviews when determining search rankings. Businesses with a higher number of positive reviews are more likely to appear at the top of search results, increasing their online visibility.

By actively encouraging customers to leave reviews, you can improve your business's search engine optimization (SEO) efforts. Positive reviews act as valuable user-generated content, which search engines consider when determining the relevance and credibility of your business.

1.2.4 Providing Valuable Feedback

Reviews, both positive and negative, provide valuable feedback for your business. Positive reviews highlight what your business is doing well and can serve as a source of motivation for your team. They provide insights into the aspects of your products or services that customers appreciate the most, allowing you to focus on those strengths.

Negative reviews, on the other hand, offer opportunities for improvement. They shed light on areas where your business may be falling short and provide valuable feedback on how to enhance the customer experience. By addressing negative reviews constructively, you can demonstrate your commitment to customer satisfaction and showcase your willingness to make necessary improvements.

1.2.5 Influencing Consumer Behavior

Reviews have a significant influence on consumer behavior. Potential customers often rely on reviews to make informed purchasing decisions. They trust the opinions and experiences of other customers more than traditional advertising or marketing messages.

Positive reviews can create a sense of urgency and FOMO (fear of missing out) among potential customers. When they see positive reviews highlighting the benefits and satisfaction others have experienced, it can create a desire to experience the same positive outcomes.

On the other hand, negative reviews can deter potential customers from engaging with your business. Addressing negative reviews promptly and professionally is crucial to mitigate any potential damage to your reputation and to reassure potential customers that you take customer satisfaction seriously.

1.2.6 Establishing a Competitive Advantage

In today's competitive business landscape, positive reviews can give your business a competitive edge. When potential customers compare your business to your competitors, positive reviews can be the deciding factor in their decision-making process. A higher number of positive reviews can differentiate your business from others and position you as the preferred choice.

By actively managing and responding to reviews, you can showcase your commitment to customer satisfaction and demonstrate your willingness to go above and beyond to address any concerns. This level of customer care can set your business apart from competitors and establish a competitive advantage.

In conclusion, the impact of reviews on business success is undeniable. Positive reviews build trust and credibility, increase sales and revenue, improve search engine rankings, provide valuable feedback, influence consumer behavior, and establish a competitive advantage. By understanding the importance of reviews and crafting effective responses, you can harness the power of stellar reviews to propel your business to new heights of success.

1.3 Why Crafting Effective Responses Matters

Crafting effective responses to reviews is a crucial aspect of managing your online reputation and building a positive brand image. When customers take the time to leave a review, whether it's positive, negative, or neutral, they are expressing their thoughts and feelings about their experience with your business. Responding to these reviews shows that you value their feedback and are committed to providing excellent customer service.

1.3.1 Building Customer Relationships

Crafting effective responses to reviews allows you to build strong relationships with your customers. When you respond to positive reviews, you have the opportunity to express your gratitude and appreciation for their kind words. This not only strengthens the bond between you and the customer but also encourages them to continue supporting your business.

Responding to negative reviews, on the other hand, gives you the chance to address any concerns or issues raised by the customer. By acknowledging their feedback and offering a solution or apology, you demonstrate your commitment to resolving problems and improving the customer experience. This can help turn a dissatisfied customer into a loyal advocate for your business.

1.3.2 Enhancing Brand Reputation

Crafting effective responses to reviews is essential for enhancing your brand reputation. Positive reviews act as testimonials for your business, and responding to them in a thoughtful and personalized manner reinforces the positive image of your brand. It shows potential customers that you value and appreciate your existing customers, which can help build trust and credibility.

Responding to negative reviews is equally important for brand reputation management. When potential customers see that you take the time to address and resolve issues, it demonstrates your commitment to customer satisfaction. It shows that you are willing to go the extra mile to ensure a positive experience, even when things don't go as planned. This can help mitigate the impact of negative reviews and showcase your dedication to providing excellent service.

1.3.3 Increasing Customer Engagement

Crafting effective responses to reviews can also increase customer engagement. When you respond to reviews, you are actively engaging with your customers and showing them that their opinions matter. This can encourage more customers to leave reviews in the future, as they see that their feedback is valued and acknowledged.

By engaging with customers through responses, you also have the opportunity to gather more information about their experiences. This can provide valuable insights into areas where you can improve your products or services. Additionally, engaging with customers publicly through responses allows other potential customers to see your commitment to customer satisfaction, which can influence their decision to choose your business.

1.3.4 Strengthening Customer Loyalty

Crafting effective responses to reviews can help strengthen customer loyalty. When customers see that you genuinely care about their feedback and take the time to respond, it creates a sense of trust and loyalty. They feel valued and appreciated, which can lead to repeat business and positive word-of-mouth recommendations.

Responding to negative reviews in a professional and empathetic manner can also help retain customers. By addressing their concerns and offering a solution, you show that you are committed to making things right. This can turn a negative experience into a positive one and reinforce the customer's trust and loyalty in your business.

1.3.5 Improving Business Operations

Crafting effective responses to reviews can provide valuable insights into areas where your business can improve. By carefully analyzing the feedback and concerns raised by customers, you can identify patterns or recurring issues. This information can help you make informed decisions about changes or improvements to your products, services, or processes.

Additionally, responding to reviews allows you to gather feedback on specific aspects of your business. Customers may highlight what they loved about their experience or suggest areas for improvement. This feedback can be used to refine your offerings and ensure that you are meeting the needs and expectations of your target audience.

In conclusion, crafting effective responses to reviews is crucial for building customer relationships, enhancing brand reputation, increasing customer engagement, strengthening customer loyalty, and improving business operations. By taking the time to respond thoughtfully and professionally to both positive and negative reviews, you can demonstrate your commitment to customer satisfaction and create a positive image for your business.

1.4 Common Challenges in Responding to Reviews

Responding to reviews is an essential part of managing your online reputation and building a positive relationship with your customers. However, it can also present some challenges that you need to be prepared for. In this section, we will explore some common challenges that businesses face when responding to reviews and provide strategies for overcoming them.

1.4.1 Balancing Timeliness and Thoughtfulness

One of the challenges in responding to reviews is finding the right balance between responding in a timely manner and providing a thoughtful and personalized response. While it is important to respond promptly to show your customers that you value their feedback, it is equally important to take the time to craft a well-thought-out response that addresses their specific concerns.

To overcome this challenge, consider setting aside dedicated time each day to respond to reviews. This will allow you to prioritize timely responses while also giving you the opportunity to carefully consider each review and provide a thoughtful response. Additionally, you can create response templates or prompts that can be customized quickly to save time while still maintaining a personal touch.

1.4.2 Dealing with Negative Emotions

Negative reviews can sometimes evoke strong emotions, especially if they contain unfair or inaccurate information. It can be challenging to respond to these reviews in a calm and professional manner. However, it is crucial to maintain a positive and empathetic tone in your responses, even when faced with criticism.

To overcome this challenge, take a step back and allow yourself some time to process your emotions before responding. Remember that your response is not only for the reviewer but also for potential customers who may be reading the review. Approach the situation with empathy and seek to understand the customer's perspective. Responding with a level-headed and understanding tone can help defuse the situation and show your commitment to resolving any issues.

1.4.3 Addressing Specific Concerns

Sometimes, reviews may contain specific concerns or complaints that require a more detailed response. It can be challenging to address these concerns effectively, especially if they involve technical or complex issues. However, it is important to provide clear and concise explanations to help the customer understand your perspective and any steps you are taking to address their concerns.

To overcome this challenge, break down the customer's concerns into smaller points and address each one individually. Use simple and jargon-free language to ensure clarity. If necessary, provide additional resources or offer to continue the conversation privately to resolve the issue. By addressing specific concerns in a thorough and transparent manner, you can demonstrate your commitment to customer satisfaction.

1.4.4 Handling Unreasonable or Unfair Reviews

Occasionally, businesses may encounter reviews that are unreasonable or unfair. These reviews can be challenging to respond to without becoming defensive or confrontational. However, it is important to maintain professionalism and address the concerns raised in a constructive manner.

To overcome this challenge, focus on the facts and avoid getting into a back-and-forth argument with the reviewer. Acknowledge their concerns, provide any relevant information or context, and offer a solution if possible. Remember that your response is not only for the reviewer but also for other potential customers who may be reading the review. By handling unreasonable or unfair reviews with grace and professionalism, you can demonstrate your commitment to excellent customer service.

1.4.5 Managing a High Volume of Reviews

As your business grows and attracts more customers, managing a high volume of reviews can become overwhelming. It can be challenging to respond to each review individually while also maintaining the quality and personalization of your responses.

To overcome this challenge, consider implementing a system for managing reviews efficiently. This can include using response templates or prompts that can be customized quickly, setting up automated email notifications for new reviews, and delegating the task of responding to reviews to a dedicated team member. By streamlining the review response process, you can ensure that each review receives a timely and thoughtful response, even in the face of a high volume of reviews.

In conclusion, responding to reviews can present various challenges for businesses. However, by being prepared and implementing strategies to overcome these challenges, you can effectively manage your online reputation and build strong relationships with your customers. Remember to balance timeliness and thoughtfulness, handle negative emotions with empathy, address specific concerns with clarity, handle unreasonable reviews professionally, and manage a high volume of reviews efficiently. With these strategies in place, you can navigate the world of reviews with confidence and maximize the benefits of stellar customer feedback.

2 Preparing for Stellar Reviews

2.1 Creating a Positive Customer Experience

Creating a positive customer experience is essential for generating stellar reviews. When customers have a positive experience with your business, they are more likely to leave glowing reviews and recommend your products or services to others. In this section, we will explore strategies and techniques for creating a positive customer experience that will lead to stellar reviews.

2.1.1 Understanding Customer Expectations

To create a positive customer experience, it is crucial to understand and meet customer expectations. Customers have certain expectations when they interact with a business, whether it's the quality of the product or service, the level of customer service, or the overall experience. By understanding these expectations, you can tailor your approach to exceed them and leave a lasting impression.

Start by conducting market research and gathering feedback from your existing customers. This will help you identify common expectations and areas where you can improve. Pay attention to customer reviews and testimonials, as they often provide valuable insights into what customers appreciate and what they expect from your business.

2.1.2 Providing Excellent Customer Service

One of the key factors in creating a positive customer experience is providing excellent customer service. Customers value businesses that are responsive, helpful, and attentive to their needs. Here are some tips for providing excellent customer service:

1. Be responsive: Respond to customer inquiries and concerns promptly. Aim to reply within 24 hours, if not sooner. This shows that you value their time and are committed to addressing their needs.
2. Be knowledgeable: Train your customer service team to have a deep understanding of your products or services. This will enable them to provide accurate and helpful information to customers.
3. Be empathetic: Show empathy towards your customers' concerns and frustrations. Put yourself in their shoes and try to understand their perspective. This will help you provide more personalized and effective solutions.
4. Go the extra mile: Look for opportunities to exceed customer expectations. Offer personalized recommendations, surprise them with a small gift or discount, or provide additional resources or information that can enhance their experience.

2.1.3 Streamlining the Customer Journey

Another important aspect of creating a positive customer experience is streamlining the customer journey. The customer journey refers to the entire process a customer goes through, from discovering your business to making a purchase and beyond. By optimizing each step of the journey, you can ensure a seamless and enjoyable experience for your customers.

Here are some strategies to streamline the customer journey:

1. Simplify the purchasing process: Make it easy for customers to find and purchase your products or services. Optimize your website or online store for a smooth checkout process, minimize the number of steps required to complete a purchase, and offer multiple payment options.
2. Provide clear and concise information: Ensure that your product descriptions, pricing, and shipping

information are clear and easy to understand. Avoid jargon or technical language that may confuse customers.

3. Offer proactive communication: Keep customers informed about the status of their order, shipping updates, and any potential delays. Proactively reach out to customers if there are any issues or changes to their order.

4. Follow up after the purchase: Send a personalized thank-you email or message after a customer makes a purchase. This not only shows appreciation but also provides an opportunity to ask for feedback or address any concerns they may have.

2.1.4 Personalizing the Customer Experience

Personalization is a powerful tool for creating a positive customer experience. Customers appreciate businesses that treat them as individuals and cater to their specific needs and preferences. Here are some ways to personalize the customer experience:

1. Collect and use customer data: Gather relevant information about your customers, such as their purchase history, preferences, and demographics. Use this data to tailor your marketing messages, recommendations, and offers.

2. Address customers by name: Whenever possible, address customers by their name in your communications. This simple gesture adds a personal touch and makes customers feel valued.

3. Offer personalized recommendations: Use customer data and purchase history to provide personalized product recommendations. This can be done through email marketing, on-site recommendations, or personalized product bundles.

4. Provide customized support: Train your customer service team to provide personalized support based on each customer's unique needs. This can involve offering tailored solutions, providing additional resources, or going above and beyond to address their concerns.

By creating a positive customer experience through excellent customer service, streamlining the customer journey, and personalizing the experience, you can set the stage for stellar reviews. Remember, happy customers are more likely to leave positive reviews and become loyal advocates for your business.

2.2 Encouraging Customers to Leave Reviews

Encouraging customers to leave reviews is a crucial aspect of building a stellar reputation for your business. Positive reviews not only boost your credibility but also attract new customers. In this section, we will explore effective strategies to encourage customers to leave reviews and share their positive experiences.

2.2.1 Providing Exceptional Customer Service

One of the most effective ways to encourage customers to leave reviews is by providing exceptional customer service. When customers have a positive experience with your business, they are more likely to share their satisfaction with others. Here are some strategies to provide exceptional customer service:

1. **Be responsive:** Respond promptly to customer inquiries and concerns. Show that you value their time and are committed to resolving any issues they may have.

2. **Go the extra mile:** Exceed customer expectations by offering personalized recommendations, providing additional information, or offering special discounts. By going above and beyond, you create a memorable experience that customers will want to share.

3. **Train your staff:** Ensure that your staff is well-trained in customer service skills. Friendly and knowledgeable employees can make a significant impact on customer satisfaction.
4. **Ask for feedback:** Regularly ask customers for feedback on their experience with your business. This not only shows that you value their opinion but also provides an opportunity for them to share their positive experiences.

2.2.2 Offering Incentives for Reviews

Incentivizing customers to leave reviews can be an effective way to encourage their participation. However, it is important to do so ethically and within the guidelines of the platform you are using. Here are some ethical ways to offer incentives for reviews:

1. **Discounts or coupons:** Offer customers a discount or coupon code for their next purchase in exchange for leaving a review. This not only encourages reviews but also incentivizes repeat business.
2. **Freebies or samples:** Provide customers with a free sample or a small gift as a token of appreciation for leaving a review. This can create a positive impression and encourage them to share their experience.
3. **Contests or giveaways:** Organize a contest or giveaway where customers can enter by leaving a review. This can generate excitement and encourage customers to participate.
4. **Loyalty program rewards:** Incorporate a review component into your loyalty program. Offer additional rewards or points for customers who leave reviews, further incentivizing their participation.

2.2.3 Simplifying the Review Process

Making the review process simple and convenient for customers can significantly increase the likelihood of them leaving a review. Here are some ways to simplify the review process:

1. **Provide clear instructions:** Clearly explain how customers can leave a review, whether it's through a specific platform, email, or your website. Provide step-by-step instructions to eliminate any confusion.
2. **Offer multiple review platforms:** Give customers the option to leave a review on different platforms, such as Google, Yelp, or social media. This allows them to choose the platform they are most comfortable with.
3. **Send follow-up emails:** After a customer makes a purchase, send a follow-up email thanking them for their business and kindly requesting a review. Include direct links to the review platforms to make it easy for them to leave a review.
4. **Create a review landing page:** Design a dedicated landing page on your website where customers can easily leave reviews. Make sure the page is user-friendly and optimized for mobile devices.

2.2.4 Leveraging Social Media and Email Marketing

Social media and email marketing can be powerful tools for encouraging customers to leave reviews. Here are some strategies to leverage these platforms effectively:

1. **Share positive reviews:** Regularly share positive reviews on your social media platforms. This not only showcases customer satisfaction but also encourages others to leave their own reviews.
2. **Run review campaigns:** Create social media or email campaigns specifically focused on encouraging customers to leave reviews. Offer incentives or discounts to those who participate.
3. **Engage with customers:** Respond to customer comments and messages on social media promptly. Engaging

with customers shows that you value their feedback and encourages them to share their experiences.
4. **Include review requests in email newsletters:** Incorporate review requests in your email newsletters. Highlight the importance of reviews and provide direct links to review platforms.

By implementing these strategies, you can effectively encourage customers to leave reviews and build a strong reputation for your business. Remember, providing exceptional customer service, offering incentives, simplifying the review process, and leveraging social media and email marketing are key elements in encouraging customers to share their positive experiences.

2.3 Monitoring and Managing Online Reputation

In today's digital age, online reputation management is crucial for businesses of all sizes. With the rise of review platforms and social media, customers have more power than ever to share their experiences and opinions about products and services. Monitoring and managing your online reputation is essential to ensure that your business maintains a positive image and builds trust with potential customers.

2.3.1 The Importance of Monitoring Online Reputation

Monitoring your online reputation involves actively tracking and analyzing what customers are saying about your business on various platforms. This includes review websites, social media platforms, forums, and even blog posts. By staying on top of your online reputation, you can quickly address any negative feedback, respond to customer concerns, and showcase your commitment to excellent customer service.

Here are a few reasons why monitoring your online reputation is essential:

1. **Customer Perception:** Your online reputation directly impacts how potential customers perceive your business. Positive reviews and feedback can attract new customers, while negative reviews can deter them. By monitoring your online reputation, you can address any negative feedback promptly and demonstrate your commitment to customer satisfaction.
2. **Brand Image:** Your online reputation is a reflection of your brand's image. Consistently positive reviews and responses can help build a strong and trustworthy brand image. On the other hand, ignoring or mishandling negative reviews can damage your brand's reputation. Monitoring your online reputation allows you to maintain a positive brand image and address any issues that may arise.
3. **Competitor Analysis:** Monitoring your online reputation also provides valuable insights into your competitors. By analyzing their reviews and customer feedback, you can identify areas where your business can improve and differentiate itself from the competition. Understanding what customers appreciate about your competitors can help you refine your own products or services.

2.3.2 Tools for Monitoring Online Reputation

To effectively monitor your online reputation, you can leverage various tools and platforms. Here are some popular options:

1. **Google Alerts:** Google Alerts is a free tool that allows you to monitor mentions of your business across the web. You can set up alerts for specific keywords, such as your business name or product names, and receive email notifications whenever those keywords are mentioned online.
2. **Social Media Listening Tools:** There are numerous social media listening tools available that allow you to

monitor mentions of your business on social media platforms. These tools provide real-time alerts and analytics, helping you stay informed about what customers are saying about your brand.

3. **Review Monitoring Platforms:** Many review monitoring platforms, such as ReviewTrackers and Brand24, offer comprehensive solutions for tracking and managing online reviews. These platforms aggregate reviews from various websites, provide sentiment analysis, and allow you to respond to reviews directly from the platform.

4. **Social Media Analytics:** Most social media platforms, such as Facebook and Twitter, provide built-in analytics tools that allow you to monitor engagement, mentions, and sentiment around your brand. These insights can help you gauge customer sentiment and identify any potential issues.

2.3.3 Responding to Online Reviews

Monitoring your online reputation is only half the battle. Responding to online reviews, both positive and negative, is equally important. When responding to reviews, keep the following tips in mind:

1. **Timeliness:** Respond to reviews promptly, ideally within 24-48 hours. This shows that you value customer feedback and are committed to addressing any concerns.

2. **Personalization:** Tailor your responses to each review. Use the customer's name if available and reference specific details from their review. This personal touch demonstrates that you genuinely care about their experience.

3. **Gratitude:** Express gratitude for positive reviews and thank customers for taking the time to share their feedback. This shows appreciation for their support and encourages them to continue advocating for your business.

4. **Empathy:** Show empathy and understanding when responding to negative reviews. Acknowledge the customer's concerns and apologize for any negative experiences they may have had. Offer a solution or invite them to contact you directly to resolve the issue.

5. **Professionalism:** Maintain a professional tone in all your responses. Avoid getting defensive or engaging in arguments with customers. Remember that your responses are public and can influence how others perceive your business.

6. **Consistency:** Be consistent in your responses across different review platforms. This helps establish a cohesive brand voice and ensures that all customers receive the same level of attention and care.

By monitoring and managing your online reputation effectively and responding to reviews in a thoughtful manner, you can build trust with your customers, enhance your brand image, and ultimately drive business success.

2.4 Setting Realistic Expectations for Reviews

When it comes to receiving reviews, it's important to set realistic expectations. As a business owner, it's natural to hope for glowing, five-star reviews from every customer. However, it's essential to understand that not every review will be perfect. In this section, we will discuss the importance of setting realistic expectations for reviews and how to handle them effectively.

2.4.1 Understanding the Nature of Reviews

Reviews are subjective opinions expressed by customers based on their personal experiences with your product or service. It's crucial to remember that not all customers will have the same expectations or preferences. Some customers may have higher standards, while others may be more forgiving. Therefore, it's unrealistic to expect every review to be flawless.

2.4.2 Embrace the Power of Constructive Criticism

Negative or critical reviews can be valuable sources of feedback for your business. Instead of viewing them as a personal attack, see them as an opportunity for growth and improvement. Constructive criticism can help you identify areas where your business can excel and make necessary changes to enhance the customer experience.

2.4.3 Encourage Honest and Balanced Reviews

While positive reviews are undoubtedly uplifting, it's important to encourage customers to provide honest and balanced feedback. Unrealistically positive reviews may raise suspicions among potential customers, who may question the authenticity of the reviews. By setting realistic expectations, you can create an environment where customers feel comfortable expressing their genuine opinions.

2.4.4 Communicate Clearly with Customers

To set realistic expectations for reviews, it's crucial to communicate clearly with your customers from the beginning. Provide accurate and detailed information about your product or service, including any limitations or potential areas for improvement. By managing customer expectations upfront, you can minimize the likelihood of disappointment and negative reviews.

2.4.5 Focus on the Overall Trend

Instead of fixating on individual reviews, it's important to focus on the overall trend of your reviews. One negative review among a sea of positive ones should not overshadow the positive feedback you receive. By analyzing the overall sentiment of your reviews, you can gain a more accurate understanding of your business's performance and make informed decisions for improvement.

2.4.6 Responding to Realistic Reviews

When responding to reviews, it's essential to acknowledge the customer's feedback and address any valid concerns they may have. By demonstrating your willingness to listen and make improvements, you can show potential customers that you value their opinions and are committed to providing an exceptional experience.

2.4.7 Avoid Overpromising

To set realistic expectations, it's crucial to avoid overpromising in your marketing materials or product descriptions. Be transparent about what your product or service can deliver and avoid making exaggerated claims. By setting realistic expectations upfront, you can minimize the likelihood of disappointment and negative reviews.

2.4.8 Learn from Negative Reviews

Negative reviews can provide valuable insights into areas where your business can improve. Take the time to analyze the feedback and identify any recurring issues or patterns. Use this information to make necessary changes and enhance the customer experience. By actively addressing concerns raised in negative reviews, you can demonstrate your commitment to continuous improvement.

2.4.9 Celebrate Positive Reviews

While it's important to set realistic expectations, it's equally important to celebrate and appreciate positive reviews. Positive reviews not only boost your business's reputation but also serve as a testament to your hard work and dedication. Take the time to thank customers for their positive feedback and let them know how much you value their support.

2.4.10 Continuous Improvement

Setting realistic expectations for reviews is an ongoing process. As your business evolves and grows, so will the expectations of your customers. Continuously monitor and analyze your reviews to identify areas for improvement and adapt your strategies accordingly. By staying proactive and responsive, you can ensure that your business consistently meets and exceeds customer expectations.

Remember, setting realistic expectations for reviews is essential for maintaining a healthy and balanced online reputation. Embrace both positive and negative feedback as opportunities for growth and improvement. By responding effectively to reviews and continuously striving for excellence, you can build a strong foundation of stellar reviews that will benefit your business in the long run.

3 Crafting Effective Responses

3.1 Understanding Different Types of Reviews

Reviews come in various forms, and as a business owner or manager, it is essential to understand the different types of reviews you may encounter. Each type requires a unique approach when crafting your responses. In this section, we will explore the various categories of reviews and provide guidance on how to effectively respond to each one.

3.1.1 Positive Reviews

Positive reviews are a cause for celebration. They not only reflect the satisfaction of your customers but also serve as powerful marketing tools for your business. When responding to positive reviews, it is crucial to show gratitude and reinforce the positive experience the customer had with your product or service.

Express Gratitude

Begin your response by expressing your sincere appreciation for the customer's positive feedback. Thank them for taking the time to share their experience and for choosing your business. This simple act of gratitude shows that you value their support and encourages them to continue supporting your brand.

Personalize the Response

Make your response personal by addressing the customer by name. This small gesture adds a personal touch and makes the customer feel valued. Additionally, reference specific details from their review to demonstrate that you have read and understood their feedback.

Highlight the Positive Aspects

Reiterate the positive aspects mentioned in the review. Emphasize the specific features, benefits, or experiences that the customer enjoyed. This not only reinforces their positive perception but also serves as a reminder to potential customers of the value your business provides.

Encourage Further Engagement

Invite the customer to engage further with your business. This could include suggesting other products or services they might be interested in, offering exclusive discounts or promotions, or inviting them to follow your social media accounts. By encouraging further engagement, you build a stronger relationship with the customer and increase the likelihood of repeat business.

3.1.2 Negative Reviews

Negative reviews can be challenging to handle, but they also present an opportunity for growth and improvement. When responding to negative reviews, it is crucial to remain calm, empathetic, and proactive in finding a resolution.

Acknowledge the Issue

Start by acknowledging the customer's concerns and frustrations. Let them know that you understand their experience and that their feedback is valuable to you. This demonstrates empathy and shows that you take their concerns seriously.

Apologize and Take Responsibility

Offer a sincere apology for any inconvenience or dissatisfaction caused. Taking responsibility for the issue shows that you are committed to resolving the problem and improving the customer's experience. Avoid making excuses or shifting blame, as this can further escalate the situation.

Provide a Solution

Offer a solution to the customer's problem or concern. This could involve providing a refund, offering a replacement product or service, or suggesting an alternative solution. Be proactive in finding a resolution that meets the customer's needs and demonstrates your commitment to their satisfaction.

Take the Conversation Offline

If the issue requires further discussion or resolution, it is best to take the conversation offline. Provide contact information or direct the customer to a specific channel where they can reach out to you directly. This allows for a more personalized and private conversation, away from the public eye.

3.1.3 Neutral or Mixed Reviews

Neutral or mixed reviews may not be as straightforward as positive or negative reviews, but they still require attention and a thoughtful response. These reviews often provide valuable feedback that can help you identify areas for improvement or address any misconceptions.

Express Appreciation

Thank the customer for their feedback, even if it is not entirely positive. Let them know that you value their input and that their review helps you understand their experience better. Expressing appreciation shows that you are open to feedback and committed to continuous improvement.

Address Specific Concerns

If the review includes specific concerns or criticisms, address them directly. Provide clarification, additional information, or context to help the customer understand your perspective. Be transparent and honest in your response, as this builds trust and credibility with the customer.

Offer Assistance or Resolution

If the review indicates that the customer encountered any issues or challenges, offer assistance or a resolution. This could involve providing additional support, offering a refund or exchange, or suggesting alternative options. By addressing their concerns, you demonstrate your commitment to customer satisfaction.

Encourage Further Feedback

Invite the customer to provide further feedback or reach out to you directly if they have any additional concerns or questions. This shows that you are open to ongoing communication and willing to address any further issues that may arise.

In the next section, we will explore the essential elements of an effective response, which can be applied to all types of reviews.

3.2 The Elements of an Effective Response

Crafting effective responses to reviews is crucial for maintaining a positive online reputation and building strong relationships with customers. When responding to reviews, whether they are positive, negative, or neutral, there are several key elements that should be included to ensure your response is effective and impactful. In this section, we will explore these elements in detail and provide you with practical tips on how to create stellar responses.

3.2.1 Personalization and Authenticity

One of the most important elements of an effective response is personalization. Customers appreciate when businesses take the time to respond to their reviews in a personalized manner. Begin your response by addressing the customer by name, if possible, and express your gratitude for their feedback. This personal touch shows that you value their opinion and are genuinely interested in their experience.

Authenticity is also crucial in crafting effective responses. Avoid using generic or automated responses as they can come across as insincere. Instead, take the time to read and understand the customer's review and respond in a genuine and heartfelt manner. This will help build trust and strengthen the customer-business relationship.

3.2.2 Acknowledgment and Appreciation

Start your response by acknowledging the customer's review and expressing your appreciation for their feedback. Let them know that their opinion matters to you and that you value their time and effort in leaving a review. This simple act of acknowledgment goes a long way in making customers feel heard and appreciated.

3.2.3 Positive Reinforcement

When responding to positive reviews, it's important to reinforce the positive aspects mentioned by the customer. Highlight specific details or experiences that the customer enjoyed and thank them for sharing their positive experience. This not only shows your appreciation but also reinforces the positive aspects of your business to potential customers who may be reading the reviews.

3.2.4 Personalized Details

To make your response more meaningful, include personalized details that reference the customer's specific experience. This could be mentioning a specific product they purchased, a service they received, or a particular interaction they had with your business. By including these personalized details, you demonstrate that you have taken the time to read and understand their review, further enhancing the authenticity of your response.

3.2.5 Offering Additional Assistance

In your response, always offer additional assistance or support to the customer. This could include providing contact information for further inquiries, offering a discount or coupon for their next purchase, or simply letting them know that you are available to address any concerns they may have. By offering this level of support, you show your commitment to customer satisfaction and build trust with both the reviewer and potential customers.

3.2.6 Professionalism and Positivity

Maintaining a professional and positive tone in your response is essential. Even if the review is negative or critical, it's important to respond in a calm and respectful manner. Avoid getting defensive or engaging in arguments. Instead, focus on addressing the customer's concerns and finding a resolution. Responding with professionalism and positivity not only reflects well on your business but also helps to diffuse any potential conflicts.

3.2.7 Timeliness

Responding to reviews in a timely manner is crucial. Aim to respond to reviews within 24-48 hours, if possible. This shows that you are actively engaged with your customers and value their feedback. Delayed responses can give the impression that you are not attentive or responsive to customer concerns, which can negatively impact your online reputation.

3.2.8 Grammar and Spelling

Pay attention to grammar and spelling when crafting your responses. Poorly written responses can give the impression of unprofessionalism and lack of attention to detail. Take the time to proofread your responses before posting them to ensure they are error-free and well-written.

3.2.9 Encouraging Further Engagement

In your response, encourage the customer to continue engaging with your business. This could include inviting them to follow your social media accounts, sign up for newsletters, or leave additional feedback in the future. By encouraging further engagement, you foster a long-term relationship with the customer and increase the likelihood of repeat business.

Crafting effective responses to reviews is an art that requires attention to detail, authenticity, and a customer-centric approach. By incorporating the elements discussed in this section, you can create responses that not only address the customer's feedback but also strengthen your brand reputation and build customer loyalty. Remember, each response is an opportunity to showcase your commitment to customer satisfaction and leave a lasting positive impression.

3.3 Addressing Positive Reviews

Positive reviews are a valuable asset for any business. They not only boost your reputation but also serve as a powerful marketing tool. When customers take the time to leave a positive review, it's important to respond in a way that shows your appreciation and reinforces their positive experience. In this section, we will explore effective strategies for addressing positive reviews and provide you with some examples to help you craft your own stellar responses.

3.3.1 Express Gratitude and Appreciation

The first step in responding to a positive review is to express your gratitude and appreciation. Let the customer know that their feedback is valued and that you are thankful for their kind words. Here's an example of how you can do this:

"Thank you so much for taking the time to leave such a wonderful review! We are thrilled to hear that you had a positive experience with our product/service. Your kind words mean a lot to us and serve as a great motivation for our team. We truly appreciate your support!"

3.3.2 Personalize Your Response

To make your response more meaningful, try to personalize it by mentioning specific details from the customer's review. This shows that you have read and understood their feedback. Here's an example:

"Dear [Customer's Name], thank you for your glowing review! We are delighted to hear that our product/service exceeded your expectations. It means a lot to us that you noticed the attention to detail we put into [specific feature mentioned by the customer]. We strive to provide the best experience possible, and your feedback encourages us to continue doing so. Thank you for choosing us!"

3.3.3 Highlight the Positive Impact

When responding to a positive review, take the opportunity to highlight the positive impact your product/service has had on the customer. This not only reinforces their positive experience but also showcases the value of your offerings to potential customers. Here's an example:

"We are thrilled to hear that our product/service has made a positive impact on your [specific aspect mentioned by the customer]. It's our goal to [describe the positive outcome]. Your feedback reassures us that we are on the right track and motivates us to keep delivering exceptional results. Thank you for sharing your experience!"

3.3.4 Encourage Repeat Business and Referrals

Positive reviews are a great opportunity to encourage repeat business and referrals. Let the customer know that you would love to serve them again in the future and that their recommendation is highly appreciated. Here's an example:

"Thank you for your kind words! We are delighted to have had the opportunity to serve you. We would love to have you as a customer again in the future and provide you with the same level of exceptional service. If you know anyone who could benefit from our product/service, we would greatly appreciate your referral. Thank you for your support!"

3.3.5 Offer a Special Discount or Promotion

To show your appreciation for a positive review, consider offering a special discount or promotion to the customer. This not only rewards their loyalty but also encourages them to continue engaging with your business. Here's an example:

"Thank you for your amazing review! We are thrilled to have you as a valued customer. As a token of our appreciation, we would like to offer you a [specific discount or promotion] on your next purchase. Simply use the code [code] at checkout to redeem your special offer. Thank you for your support!"

3.3.6 Keep it Professional and Genuine

When crafting your response, it's important to maintain a professional and genuine tone. Avoid using generic or automated responses and instead, take the time to personalize your message. This shows that you genuinely care about your customers and their feedback. Here's an example:

"Dear [Customer's Name], thank you for your wonderful review! We are thrilled to hear that you had a positive experience with our product/service. Your kind words mean a lot to us and serve as a great motivation for our team. We truly appreciate your support and look forward to serving you again in the future. Thank you!"

Remember, addressing positive reviews is an opportunity to strengthen your relationship with customers and showcase your commitment to excellence. By expressing gratitude, personalizing your response, highlighting the positive impact, encouraging repeat business and referrals, offering special discounts or promotions, and maintaining a professional and genuine tone, you can create meaningful connections with your customers and turn positive experiences into long-term loyalty.

Now that we have explored effective strategies for addressing positive reviews, let's move on to the next section, where we will discuss how to respond to negative reviews.

3.4 Responding to Negative Reviews

Negative reviews can be disheartening and challenging to deal with, but they also present an opportunity for growth and improvement. How you respond to these reviews can have a significant impact on your business's reputation and customer perception. In this section, we will explore effective strategies for responding to negative reviews and turning them into positive experiences.

3.4.1 Acknowledge and Empathize

When responding to a negative review, it is crucial to acknowledge the customer's concerns and show empathy towards their experience. Begin your response by thanking the customer for their feedback and expressing your understanding of their disappointment or frustration. This initial step sets the tone for a constructive conversation and demonstrates your commitment to addressing their concerns.

3.4.2 Take the Conversation Offline

While it is essential to respond to negative reviews publicly, it is equally important to take the conversation offline to resolve the issue privately. Provide contact information or a direct message option where the customer can reach out to you directly. This approach shows that you are genuinely interested in resolving the problem and provides an opportunity for a more personalized and effective solution.

3.4.3 Offer a Solution or Compensation

In your response, offer a solution or compensation that addresses the customer's specific concerns. This could involve offering a refund, replacement, or any other appropriate resolution. By providing a tangible solution, you demonstrate your commitment to customer satisfaction and your willingness to make things right.

3.4.4 Apologize and Take Responsibility

Apologizing for any negative experience the customer had is a crucial step in responding to negative reviews. Even if the issue was beyond your control, expressing regret and taking responsibility for the situation shows that you value the customer's feedback and are committed to improving their experience. Avoid making excuses or shifting blame, as this can further escalate the situation.

3.4.5 Maintain Professionalism and Stay Calm

It is essential to maintain professionalism and stay calm when responding to negative reviews, regardless of the tone or language used by the customer. Responding with anger or defensiveness will only worsen the situation and reflect poorly on your business. Keep your response concise, respectful, and focused on finding a resolution.

3.4.6 Address the Issue and Provide Explanations

In your response, address the specific issues raised in the negative review. Provide explanations or clarifications where necessary, but be careful not to sound defensive. Use this opportunity to educate the customer about any misunderstandings or miscommunications that may have occurred. By addressing the issue directly, you show your commitment to transparency and customer satisfaction.

3.4.7 Follow Up and Seek Feedback

After resolving the issue, follow up with the customer to ensure their satisfaction and ask for feedback on the resolution process. This step demonstrates your dedication to continuous improvement and shows that you value their opinion. By seeking feedback, you can identify areas for improvement and prevent similar issues from arising in the future.

3.4.8 Learn from Negative Reviews

Negative reviews can provide valuable insights into areas where your business can improve. Take the time to analyze the feedback and identify any recurring themes or patterns. Use this information to make necessary changes to your products, services, or processes. By learning from negative reviews, you can turn them into opportunities for growth and enhance the overall customer experience.

3.4.9 Respond Promptly and Consistently

Timely responses to negative reviews are crucial to demonstrate your commitment to customer satisfaction. Aim to respond within 24-48 hours to show that you take feedback seriously and are actively working towards a resolution. Consistency in your responses is also important, as it helps build trust and credibility with your customers.

3.4.10 Monitor and Address Fake or Malicious Reviews

Unfortunately, not all negative reviews are genuine. Some may be fake or malicious attempts to harm your business's reputation. It is essential to monitor your reviews regularly and identify any suspicious patterns or reviews that violate the platform's policies. If you suspect a review is fake or malicious, reach out to the platform's support team and provide evidence to have it removed.

Remember, negative reviews are an opportunity for growth and improvement. By responding effectively and addressing customer concerns, you can turn a negative experience into a positive one. Your professionalism, empathy, and commitment to customer satisfaction will not only resolve the immediate issue but also showcase your dedication to providing stellar experiences for all customers.

3.5 Dealing with Neutral or Mixed Reviews

Receiving neutral or mixed reviews can be a bit challenging for businesses. Unlike positive reviews that boost your confidence and negative reviews that provide an opportunity for improvement, neutral or mixed reviews can leave you feeling uncertain about how to respond. However, these reviews are still valuable and should be addressed in a thoughtful and professional manner. In this section, we will explore strategies for dealing with neutral or mixed reviews and provide you with some examples to help you craft effective responses.

3.5.1 Acknowledge the Feedback

When responding to neutral or mixed reviews, it's important to acknowledge the feedback and show appreciation for the customer's time and effort in leaving a review. Begin your response by thanking the customer for their feedback and expressing your gratitude for their support. This simple act of acknowledgment can go a long way in building a positive relationship with the customer.

Example response: "Thank you for taking the time to share your feedback with us. We appreciate your support and value your opinion."

3.5.2 Seek Clarification

Neutral or mixed reviews often lack specific details or may be unclear about the customer's concerns. In such cases, it's essential to seek clarification to better understand the customer's experience. Ask open-ended questions to encourage the customer to provide more information about their concerns. This will not only help you address their issues but also demonstrate your commitment to resolving any potential problems.

Example response: "We appreciate your feedback and would like to learn more about your experience. Could you please provide us with additional details so that we can better understand your concerns and work towards a resolution?"

3.5.3 Apologize and Offer Solutions

Even if the review is not entirely negative, it's crucial to apologize for any inconvenience or dissatisfaction the customer may have experienced. Show empathy and understanding towards their concerns. Offer solutions or alternatives to address their issues and demonstrate your commitment to customer satisfaction. Providing options shows that you are willing to go the extra mile to make things right.

Example response: "We apologize for any inconvenience you may have experienced. We understand your concerns and would like to offer you [specific solution or alternative]. We hope this will help resolve the issue and provide you with a better experience in the future."

3.5.4 Highlight Positive Aspects

While addressing the customer's concerns, it's essential to highlight any positive aspects of their review. This not only shows that you have carefully considered their feedback but also helps to balance the overall tone of your response. By acknowledging the positive aspects, you can reinforce the customer's trust in your business and emphasize your commitment to continuous improvement.

Example response: "We appreciate your feedback and are glad to hear that you found [specific positive aspect]. We understand your concerns and will take them into consideration as we strive to improve our [product/service]. Thank you for bringing this to our attention."

3.5.5 Offer a Follow-up

In some cases, it may be necessary to offer a follow-up to address the customer's concerns more effectively. This could involve scheduling a call, arranging a meeting, or providing additional assistance. By offering a follow-up, you demonstrate your commitment to resolving the issue and ensuring the customer's satisfaction. Be sure to provide clear instructions on how the customer can reach out to you for further assistance.

Example response: "We appreciate your feedback and would like to offer a follow-up to address your concerns more effectively. Please feel free to reach out to our customer support team at [contact information] so that we can further assist you. We value your business and want to ensure your complete satisfaction."

3.5.6 Stay Professional and Positive

Regardless of the nature of the review, it's crucial to maintain a professional and positive tone in your response. Avoid becoming defensive or engaging in arguments with the customer. Instead, focus on finding a resolution and providing exceptional customer service. Remember, your response is not only for the reviewer but also for potential customers who may be reading the review and your response.

Example response: "Thank you for sharing your feedback with us. We appreciate your honesty and are committed to addressing your concerns. We value your business and will do everything we can to ensure your satisfaction."

3.5.7 Monitor and Learn from Neutral or Mixed Reviews

Neutral or mixed reviews can provide valuable insights into areas where your business can improve. Take the opportunity to analyze these reviews and identify any patterns or recurring issues. Use this feedback to make necessary adjustments to your products, services, or customer experience. By continuously learning from these reviews, you can enhance your business and strive for excellence.

Example response: "We appreciate your feedback and will take it into consideration as we continue to improve our [product/service]. Your insights are valuable to us, and we are committed to providing the best possible experience for our customers. Thank you for helping us grow."

Remember, every review, whether positive, negative, or neutral, is an opportunity to engage with your customers and demonstrate your commitment to their satisfaction. By responding thoughtfully and professionally to neutral or mixed reviews, you can turn potential challenges into opportunities for growth and improvement.

3.6 Handling Reviews with Specific Concerns

In this section, we will explore how to handle reviews with specific concerns. While positive reviews are always a joy to receive, it's important to address any concerns or issues raised in reviews to maintain customer satisfaction and demonstrate your commitment to excellent customer service. This section will provide you with strategies and examples for effectively responding to reviews with specific concerns.

3.6.1 Addressing Shipping and Delivery Concerns

One common concern that customers may raise in their reviews is related to shipping and delivery. Whether it's a delay in delivery, damaged packaging, or any other shipping-related issue, it's crucial to address these concerns promptly and professionally. Here are some tips for handling reviews with shipping and delivery concerns:

1. **Acknowledge the concern**: Start by acknowledging the customer's concern and apologize for any inconvenience caused. Let them know that you take their feedback seriously and are committed to resolving

the issue.

2. **Offer a solution**: Depending on the specific concern, offer a suitable solution to address the problem. This could include offering a replacement, refund, or any other appropriate resolution. Be sure to communicate the steps you will take to rectify the situation.
3. **Provide reassurance**: Reassure the customer that steps will be taken to prevent similar issues in the future. Highlight any measures you have in place to improve your shipping and delivery processes.

Example response:

Dear [Customer's Name],

Thank you for bringing the shipping delay to our attention. We sincerely apologize for any inconvenience this may have caused. We understand the importance of timely delivery and are committed to resolving this issue.

To make it right, we will expedite the shipping of your order and provide you with a tracking number within the next 24 hours. We assure you that we are taking steps to improve our shipping processes to prevent such delays in the future.

Once again, we apologize for any inconvenience caused and appreciate your understanding.

Best regards,

[Your Name]

3.6.2 Handling Product Quality Concerns

Another common concern that customers may express in their reviews is related to product quality. Whether it's a defect, poor craftsmanship, or any other issue with the product itself, addressing these concerns is crucial to maintaining customer satisfaction. Here's how you can handle reviews with product quality concerns:

1. **Express empathy**: Start by expressing empathy and understanding towards the customer's concern. Let them know that you value their feedback and are committed to resolving the issue.
2. **Offer a solution**: Depending on the specific concern, offer a suitable solution to address the problem. This could include offering a replacement, repair, or refund. Clearly communicate the steps you will take to rectify the situation.
3. **Highlight quality control measures**: Assure the customer that you have quality control measures in place to prevent similar issues in the future. Share any relevant information about your manufacturing process or quality assurance procedures.

Example response:

Dear [Customer's Name],

Thank you for bringing the issue with the product quality to our attention. We sincerely apologize for any disappointment this may have caused. We value your feedback and are committed to resolving this issue.

To make it right, we will send you a replacement product immediately. We have also taken steps to improve our quality control measures to prevent similar issues in the future.

Once again, we apologize for any inconvenience caused and appreciate your understanding.

Best regards,

[Your Name]

3.6.3 Responding to Customer Service Concerns

Sometimes, customers may express concerns related to their experience with your customer service. It's important to address these concerns promptly and professionally to demonstrate your commitment to excellent customer service. Here's how you can handle reviews with customer service concerns:

1. **Apologize and empathize**: Start by apologizing for any negative experience the customer had with your customer service. Express empathy and let them know that you take their feedback seriously.
2. **Investigate and rectify**: Look into the specific concern raised by the customer and take appropriate steps to rectify the situation. This may involve retraining staff, improving communication processes, or any other necessary actions.
3. **Reassure and offer assistance**: Reassure the customer that their feedback has been taken seriously and that measures have been implemented to prevent similar issues in the future. Offer your assistance in resolving any outstanding concerns they may have.

Example response:

Dear [Customer's Name],

We are truly sorry to hear about your negative experience with our customer service. We apologize for any frustration or inconvenience caused. Your feedback is invaluable to us, and we appreciate you bringing this to our attention.

We have investigated the matter thoroughly and have taken immediate steps to address the issues raised. Our team has undergone additional training to ensure better communication and resolution of customer concerns.

If there are any outstanding concerns you would like us to address, please do not hesitate to reach out to us directly. We are here to assist you and ensure your complete satisfaction.

Once again, we apologize for any inconvenience caused and appreciate your understanding.

Best regards,

[Your Name]

Remember, addressing specific concerns raised in reviews is an opportunity to showcase your commitment to customer satisfaction and continuous improvement. By responding promptly, professionally, and offering suitable solutions, you can turn a potentially negative experience into a positive one for both the customer and your business.

4 Using Templates and Examples

4.1 The Benefits of Using Response Templates

Using response templates can be a valuable tool for businesses when it comes to crafting effective responses to positive reviews. These templates provide a structured framework that can save time and ensure consistency in your responses. In this section, we will explore the benefits of using response templates and how they can enhance your overall review management strategy.

4.1.1 Time-saving and Efficiency

One of the primary benefits of using response templates is the time-saving aspect. As a business owner or manager, you likely receive numerous positive reviews on a regular basis. Responding to each review individually can be time-consuming, especially when you have other tasks to attend to. By utilizing response templates, you can streamline the process and respond to reviews more efficiently.

Templates allow you to have pre-written responses ready to go, which can be easily customized to fit the specific review. This eliminates the need to start from scratch every time you receive a positive review. With just a few tweaks, you can personalize the response and send it off in a matter of minutes. This time-saving aspect is particularly beneficial for businesses that receive a high volume of positive reviews.

4.1.2 Consistency and Brand Voice

Maintaining consistency in your responses is crucial for building a strong brand image. Response templates help ensure that your replies to positive reviews are consistent in tone, style, and messaging. This consistency reinforces your brand voice and helps create a cohesive customer experience.

By using templates, you can establish a set of key messages and phrases that align with your brand values. This consistency not only helps in managing your online reputation but also reinforces your brand identity. Customers will recognize and appreciate the consistent voice and messaging across all your responses, which can contribute to building trust and loyalty.

4.1.3 Professionalism and Politeness

Crafting responses that are professional and polite is essential when engaging with customers online. Response templates can assist in maintaining a high level of professionalism and ensuring that your replies are consistently polite and respectful.

Templates provide a framework that guides your responses, helping you avoid any potential miscommunication or misunderstandings. They can help you strike the right balance between being friendly and professional, ensuring that your responses are well-received by customers.

4.1.4 Personalization and Customization

While response templates offer a structured framework, they also allow for personalization and customization. Each positive review is unique, and it's important to acknowledge and appreciate the specific feedback provided by the customer.

Templates can serve as a starting point, providing a structure for your response. From there, you can tailor the message to address the specific details mentioned in the review. This personalization shows that you genuinely value and appreciate the customer's feedback, enhancing the overall customer experience.

4.1.5 Consistent Messaging and Brand Promotion

Response templates can also be used to consistently promote your brand and its offerings. By including key messages or information about your business in your responses, you can reinforce your brand's value proposition and encourage further engagement.

For example, you can highlight any ongoing promotions, upcoming events, or new product launches in your responses. This not only keeps customers informed but also helps drive additional sales and engagement. Response templates provide a convenient way to consistently promote your brand and its unique selling points.

4.1.6 Training and Onboarding

Response templates can be particularly useful for training new team members or onboarding employees who are responsible for managing reviews. By providing them with a set of templates, you can ensure that they have a clear understanding of the brand voice and messaging.

Templates serve as a guide for new team members, helping them respond to positive reviews in a manner that aligns with your brand's values. This consistency in responses across your team members helps maintain a unified brand image and ensures that customers receive a consistent experience, regardless of who is responding to their reviews.

In conclusion, using response templates for positive reviews offers several benefits, including time-saving, consistency, professionalism, personalization, and brand promotion. By leveraging these templates, businesses can efficiently manage their online reputation, reinforce their brand identity, and provide a positive customer experience.

4.2 Customizing Templates for Your Business

When it comes to crafting effective responses to positive reviews, having a template can be incredibly helpful. Templates provide a framework that you can customize to fit your business's unique voice and style. In this section, we will explore how you can customize templates for your business to ensure that your responses to positive reviews are authentic and personalized.

4.2.1 Understanding Your Brand Voice

Before customizing templates, it's important to have a clear understanding of your brand voice. Your brand voice is the personality and tone that you want to convey to your customers. It should align with your overall brand identity and values. Take some time to define your brand voice by considering the following questions:

- What adjectives would you use to describe your brand?
- How do you want your customers to perceive your business?
- What emotions do you want to evoke in your customers?
- What is the overall tone you want to convey in your communications?

By understanding your brand voice, you can ensure that your responses to positive reviews are consistent with your overall brand image.

4.2.2 Personalizing Templates

While templates provide a starting point, it's important to personalize your responses to make them feel genuine and heartfelt. Here are some tips for customizing templates for your business:

1. Use the customer's name: Addressing the customer by name adds a personal touch to your response. It shows that you value their individual experience and appreciate their feedback.
2. Reference specific details: Take note of any specific details mentioned in the review and incorporate them into your response. This shows that you have read and understood their feedback, making the response more personalized.
3. Express gratitude: Begin your response by expressing gratitude for the customer's positive review. Let them know that you appreciate their support and value their business.
4. Highlight the positive aspects: Acknowledge the specific positive aspects mentioned in the review and emphasize them in your response. This shows that you are attentive to your customers' needs and reinforces the positive experience they had.
5. Share your enthusiasm: Show genuine enthusiasm and excitement in your response. Let the customer know that their positive review has made your day and that you are thrilled to have provided them with a great experience.
6. Offer a personalized invitation: Encourage the customer to continue their relationship with your business by offering a personalized invitation. This could be an invitation to visit your store again, try out new products, or join your loyalty program.

Remember, the key to personalizing templates is to make the response feel authentic and tailored to the individual customer. Avoid using generic or robotic language that may come across as insincere.

4.2.3 Adapting Templates for Different Platforms

It's important to adapt your templates for different review platforms. Each platform may have its own guidelines and character limits, so make sure to tailor your responses accordingly. Here are some platform-specific considerations:

1. Etsy: If you are responding to reviews on Etsy, keep in mind the platform's community guidelines and policies. Etsy encourages sellers to respond to reviews in a professional and respectful manner. Make sure to address any specific concerns mentioned in the review and offer solutions if necessary.
2. Google Reviews: When responding to Google Reviews, keep your responses concise and to the point. Google Reviews often have character limits, so make sure to prioritize the most important information in your response.
3. Social Media: If you receive positive reviews on social media platforms like Facebook or Instagram, take advantage of the platform's features. You can use emojis, GIFs, or even share a photo to make your response more engaging and visually appealing.

Adapting your templates for different platforms shows that you are attentive to the specific needs and expectations of each platform's audience.

4.2.4 Testing and Refining Your Templates

Once you have customized your templates, it's important to test and refine them over time. Pay attention to the responses you receive from customers and make adjustments as needed. Here are some tips for testing and refining your templates:

1. Monitor customer feedback: Keep track of the responses you receive from customers and look for patterns or trends. This will help you identify areas where your templates may need improvement.
2. Seek feedback from your team: If you have a team of customer service representatives, ask for their input on the templates. They may have valuable insights and suggestions for improvement.
3. Continuously update your templates: As your business evolves, your templates should evolve too. Make sure to regularly review and update your templates to reflect any changes in your brand voice or customer expectations.

By continuously testing and refining your templates, you can ensure that your responses to positive reviews are always effective and aligned with your business goals.

In the next section, we will provide examples of stellar responses to positive reviews to further guide you in customizing your own templates.

Now that you have a better understanding of how to customize templates for your business, let's move on to the next section: "Examples of Stellar Responses to Positive Reviews."

4.3 Examples of Stellar Responses to Positive Reviews

Positive reviews are a valuable asset for any business. They not only boost your reputation but also serve as a powerful marketing tool. Responding to positive reviews is just as important as responding to negative ones. It shows your appreciation for the customer's feedback and helps build a strong relationship with them. In this section, we will provide you with some examples of stellar responses to positive reviews that you can use as a template for your own business.

4.3.1 Expressing Gratitude and Appreciation

When responding to positive reviews, it is essential to express your gratitude and appreciation for the customer's feedback. Here are a few examples:

- "Thank you so much for your kind words! We are thrilled to hear that you had a great experience with our product/service. Your satisfaction is our top priority, and we are grateful for your support."

- "We are delighted to receive your positive review! It means a lot to us that you took the time to share your experience. We strive to provide the best quality products/services, and your feedback encourages us to keep up the good work."

- "Wow! Thank you for the amazing review! We are overjoyed to hear that our product/service exceeded your expectations. Your satisfaction is what drives us, and we are grateful for your support."

4.3.2 Personalizing the Response

Adding a personal touch to your response can make the customer feel valued and appreciated. Here are a few examples:

- "Hi [Customer Name], thank you so much for your wonderful review! We are thrilled to hear that you loved our product/service. It was a pleasure serving you, and we look forward to assisting you with any future needs."

- "Dear [Customer Name], we can't thank you enough for your kind words! It means a lot to us that you had such a positive experience with our business. We are committed to providing excellent customer service, and we are here for you whenever you need us."

- "Hello [Customer Name], we are absolutely thrilled to receive your glowing review! Your satisfaction is our ultimate goal, and we are delighted to have met your expectations. We appreciate your support and look forward to serving you again soon."

4.3.3 Highlighting Specific Aspects

If the customer mentions specific aspects of your product or service in their review, acknowledge and highlight those points in your response. Here are a few examples:

- "Thank you for highlighting our prompt delivery service in your review! We understand the importance of timely delivery, and we are glad that we could meet your expectations. Your satisfaction is our priority, and we appreciate your feedback."

- "We are thrilled that you found our customer support team helpful and responsive! Providing excellent customer service is one of our core values, and we are glad that we could assist you. Thank you for your kind words and for choosing our business."

- "We are delighted that you enjoyed the unique design of our product! Our team works hard to create innovative and eye-catching designs, and we are thrilled that it resonated with you. Your positive feedback motivates us to continue pushing the boundaries of creativity."

4.3.4 Encouraging Future Engagement

When responding to positive reviews, it is an excellent opportunity to encourage future engagement and repeat business. Here are a few examples:

- "Thank you for your positive review! We would love to serve you again in the future. Don't hesitate to reach out if you have any further questions or need assistance. We value your business and look forward to being of service to you again."

- "We are grateful for your support and would love to have you as a returning customer. Keep an eye out for our upcoming promotions and new product releases. We appreciate your feedback and hope to see you again soon."

- "Your positive review means the world to us! We would be thrilled if you could share your experience with your friends and family. Word-of-mouth recommendations are invaluable to us, and we appreciate your support in spreading the word about our business."

Remember, when responding to positive reviews, always keep your tone genuine, friendly, and professional. Each response should be personalized to the customer and reflect your brand's voice. Use these examples as a starting point and customize them to fit your business and customer's specific feedback.

Now that we have covered examples of stellar responses to positive reviews, let's move on to the next chapter, where we will explore effective responses to negative reviews.

4.4 Examples of Effective Responses to Negative Reviews

Negative reviews can be challenging to handle, but they also present an opportunity to showcase your excellent customer service and willingness to address concerns. Responding effectively to negative reviews can help turn a dissatisfied customer into a loyal advocate for your business. In this section, we will provide you with examples of effective responses to negative reviews, along with some tips on how to handle them.

4.4.1 Acknowledge the Customer's Concerns

When responding to a negative review, it's crucial to acknowledge the customer's concerns and show empathy. Here's an example:

"Dear [Customer's Name],

Thank you for taking the time to share your feedback. We are sorry to hear about your experience and understand your frustration. We strive to provide the best possible service, and we apologize for falling short in this instance.

We would like to address your concerns and make things right. Could you please provide us with more details about your specific issue? We want to ensure that we fully understand the situation and take appropriate action.

Thank you for bringing this to our attention, and we look forward to resolving this matter for you.

Best regards, [Your Name]"

By acknowledging the customer's concerns and expressing a genuine desire to resolve the issue, you show that you value their feedback and are committed to improving their experience.

4.4.2 Offer a Solution or Compensation

In some cases, it may be appropriate to offer a solution or compensation to the customer to rectify their negative experience. Here's an example:

"Dear [Customer's Name],

We appreciate your feedback and apologize for the inconvenience you experienced. We understand how frustrating it can be when things don't go as expected.

To make it right, we would like to offer you [specific solution or compensation]. We believe this will address your concerns and provide a satisfactory resolution. Please let us know if this works for you, or if you have any other suggestions on how we can improve your experience.

Once again, we apologize for any inconvenience caused and appreciate your understanding.

Best regards, [Your Name]"

By offering a solution or compensation, you demonstrate your commitment to customer satisfaction and your willingness to go above and beyond to resolve the issue.

4.4.3 Take the Conversation Offline

In some cases, it may be more appropriate to take the conversation offline to address the customer's concerns privately. Here's an example:

"Dear [Customer's Name],

Thank you for bringing this matter to our attention. We apologize for any inconvenience caused and would like to resolve this issue promptly.

To ensure we can address your concerns effectively, we kindly request that you contact our customer support team at [contact information]. Our dedicated team will be more than happy to assist you and find a suitable solution.

We value your feedback and appreciate your understanding. We look forward to hearing from you soon.

Best regards, [Your Name]"

By taking the conversation offline, you provide a more personalized and private channel for resolving the issue, showing the customer that their concerns are being taken seriously.

4.4.4 Follow Up and Confirm Resolution

After addressing the customer's concerns, it's essential to follow up and confirm that the issue has been resolved to their satisfaction. Here's an example:

"Dear [Customer's Name],

We would like to follow up on the issue you raised in your review. We sincerely apologize for any inconvenience caused and want to ensure that we have resolved the matter to your satisfaction.

Could you please confirm if the [solution or compensation offered] has met your expectations? If there is anything else we can do to improve your experience, please let us know.

Thank you for your understanding and for giving us the opportunity to make things right.

Best regards, [Your Name]"

By following up and confirming the resolution, you demonstrate your commitment to customer satisfaction and show that you value their feedback even after the initial response.

4.4.5 Stay Professional and Positive

Regardless of the nature of the negative review, it's crucial to maintain a professional and positive tone in your response. Avoid getting defensive or engaging in arguments. Instead, focus on finding a resolution and providing excellent customer service.

Remember, your response is not only for the reviewer but also for potential customers who may be reading the review. By handling negative reviews with professionalism and positivity, you can showcase your commitment to customer satisfaction and build trust with your audience.

Conclusion

Responding effectively to negative reviews is an essential aspect of managing your online reputation and maintaining customer satisfaction. By acknowledging the customer's concerns, offering solutions or compensation, taking the conversation offline when necessary, following up, and maintaining a professional tone, you can turn negative experiences into positive outcomes.

Remember, negative reviews provide an opportunity to learn and improve your business. Use them as constructive feedback to identify areas for growth and make necessary changes. By addressing negative reviews with care and attention, you can demonstrate your commitment to customer satisfaction and build a strong and reputable brand.

5 Etsy and Business Specifics

5.1 Leveraging Etsy for Stellar Reviews

Etsy is a popular online marketplace that provides a platform for artisans, crafters, and small business owners to sell their unique products. With millions of active buyers and sellers, Etsy offers a great opportunity for businesses to receive stellar reviews and build a strong reputation. In this section, we will explore how you can leverage Etsy to generate positive reviews and enhance your business's success.

5.1.1 Understanding Etsy's Review System

Before diving into the strategies for obtaining stellar reviews on Etsy, it is crucial to understand how the platform's review system works. Etsy allows buyers to leave reviews for their purchases, rating the product and the overall buying experience on a scale of one to five stars. These reviews are visible to other potential buyers and can greatly influence their purchasing decisions.

Etsy's review system is designed to be transparent and fair. Sellers have the opportunity to respond to reviews, providing them with a chance to address any concerns or express gratitude for positive feedback. This interaction between sellers and buyers is an essential aspect of building a strong reputation on Etsy.

5.1.2 Encouraging Positive Reviews on Etsy

Receiving positive reviews on Etsy can significantly impact your business's success. Positive reviews not only attract more customers but also build trust and credibility. Here are some strategies to encourage positive reviews on Etsy:

1. Provide exceptional customer service: Delivering outstanding customer service is key to receiving positive reviews. Respond promptly to customer inquiries, provide accurate product descriptions, and ensure timely shipping.
2. Offer high-quality products: Consistently delivering high-quality products will leave a lasting impression on your customers. Pay attention to detail, use quality materials, and strive for excellence in every aspect of your business.
3. Personalize the buying experience: Make your customers feel special by adding personal touches to their orders. Include handwritten thank-you notes, offer customization options, or provide small surprises with each purchase.
4. Follow up with customers: After a customer receives their order, follow up with them to ensure their satisfaction. Send a friendly email or message asking for feedback and offering assistance if needed.
5. Provide clear and accurate product information: Avoid any misunderstandings or disappointments by providing detailed and accurate product descriptions, including measurements, materials used, and any customization options.
6. Offer incentives for reviews: Consider offering a small discount or a free gift to customers who leave a review. This can motivate them to share their positive experiences and increase the likelihood of receiving stellar reviews.

5.1.3 Responding to Etsy Reviews

Crafting effective responses to Etsy reviews is crucial for maintaining a positive image and building customer loyalty. Here are some tips for responding to different types of Etsy reviews:

5.1.3.1 Addressing Positive Reviews

When responding to positive reviews, express your gratitude and appreciation for the customer's feedback. Here's an example response:

"Thank you so much for your kind words! We are thrilled to hear that you love your [product name]. It was a pleasure serving you, and we look forward to creating more beautiful products for you in the future. Thank you for supporting our small business!"

5.1.3.2 Responding to Negative Reviews

Negative reviews can be challenging, but they also provide an opportunity to showcase your excellent customer service. When responding to negative reviews, follow these guidelines:

1. Remain calm and professional: It's essential to respond to negative reviews in a calm and professional manner. Avoid getting defensive or engaging in an argument. Instead, focus on finding a solution and addressing the customer's concerns.
2. Apologize and empathize: Start by apologizing for the customer's negative experience and expressing empathy for their frustration. Acknowledge their concerns and assure them that you are committed to resolving the issue.
3. Offer a solution: Propose a solution to the customer's problem. This could involve offering a refund, a replacement product, or any other appropriate resolution. Be proactive in finding a solution that satisfies the customer.
4. Take the conversation offline: To maintain privacy and resolve the issue more effectively, encourage the customer to contact you privately through Etsy's messaging system or provide an email address for further communication.

Here's an example response to a negative review:

"We are sorry to hear about your experience with our [product name]. We apologize for any inconvenience caused and understand your frustration. We would like to make it right for you. Please reach out to us through Etsy's messaging system, and we will work together to find a solution that meets your satisfaction. Thank you for bringing this to our attention."

5.1.3.3 Dealing with Neutral or Mixed Reviews

Neutral or mixed reviews may not be as straightforward as positive or negative reviews. When responding to these reviews, focus on addressing any specific concerns mentioned by the customer and offering assistance if needed. Here's an example response:

"Thank you for taking the time to leave a review. We appreciate your feedback and would love to learn more about your experience. Please reach out to us through Etsy's messaging system so that we can address any concerns you may have. We value your satisfaction and are committed to providing the best possible experience for our customers."

5.1.4 Tips for Managing Etsy Reviews

Managing your Etsy reviews effectively is crucial for maintaining a stellar reputation. Here are some additional tips to help you navigate the review process on Etsy:

1. Monitor your reviews regularly: Stay on top of your reviews by checking your Etsy account frequently. Respond promptly to both positive and negative reviews to show your commitment to customer satisfaction.
2. Be authentic and genuine: When responding to reviews, be authentic and genuine in your tone. Personalize your responses and show appreciation for each customer's feedback.
3. Learn from feedback: Use reviews as an opportunity to learn and improve your products and services. Pay attention to recurring themes or concerns mentioned in reviews and take steps to address them.
4. Encourage customers to update their reviews: If you successfully resolve a customer's issue, kindly ask them to update their review to reflect their updated experience. This can help mitigate the impact of a negative review.

By leveraging Etsy effectively, you can generate stellar reviews that will enhance your business's success. Remember to provide exceptional customer service, encourage positive reviews, and respond to reviews in a professional and empathetic manner. With these strategies in place, you can build a strong reputation on Etsy and attract more customers to your business.

5.2 Understanding Etsy's Review Policies

Etsy is a popular online marketplace that allows individuals and businesses to sell handmade, vintage, and unique items. As a seller on Etsy, it is important to understand the platform's review policies in order to effectively respond to customer reviews. Etsy's review policies are designed to ensure transparency, fairness, and trust within the marketplace. In this section, we will explore the key aspects of Etsy's review policies and how they impact your ability to respond to reviews.

5.2.1 The Importance of Authentic Reviews

Etsy places a high value on authentic reviews. They believe that honest and unbiased feedback is crucial for maintaining the integrity of the marketplace. To ensure the authenticity of reviews, Etsy has implemented several policies:

1. **Only Buyers Can Leave Reviews**: Etsy allows only customers who have made a purchase to leave a review. This policy ensures that reviews come from genuine buyers who have firsthand experience with the product or service.
2. **No Incentivized Reviews**: Etsy prohibits sellers from offering incentives, such as discounts or freebies, in exchange for positive reviews. This policy aims to prevent biased or manipulated feedback.
3. **No Review Manipulation**: Sellers are not allowed to manipulate or coerce buyers into leaving positive reviews. This includes actions such as threatening negative consequences for not leaving a positive review.

By adhering to these policies, Etsy aims to maintain a trustworthy and reliable review system that benefits both buyers and sellers.

5.2.2 The Role of Sellers in Review Responses

As a seller on Etsy, you have the opportunity to respond to customer reviews. Your responses can have a significant impact on your reputation and the perception of your business. However, it is important to understand the guidelines set by Etsy when crafting your responses:

1. **Professional and Respectful Tone**: Etsy expects sellers to maintain a professional and respectful tone in their responses. Avoid using offensive language or engaging in arguments with customers. Instead, focus on addressing the customer's concerns and providing helpful information.
2. **No Personal Information**: Etsy prohibits sellers from sharing personal information, such as phone numbers or email addresses, in their review responses. This policy is in place to protect the privacy and security of both buyers and sellers.
3. **Avoid Self-Promotion**: While it is acceptable to thank customers for their positive reviews, Etsy discourages excessive self-promotion in review responses. Instead, focus on expressing gratitude and addressing any specific feedback mentioned in the review.

By following these guidelines, you can ensure that your review responses align with Etsy's policies and contribute to a positive customer experience.

5.2.3 Handling Negative Reviews on Etsy

Negative reviews can be challenging for any seller, but it is important to approach them with professionalism and empathy. Etsy provides some guidance on how to handle negative reviews:

1. **Take Time to Reflect**: Before responding to a negative review, take a moment to gather your thoughts and emotions. It is important to respond in a calm and collected manner.
2. **Acknowledge the Customer's Concerns**: Start your response by acknowledging the customer's concerns and expressing empathy. Let them know that you understand their frustration and are committed to resolving the issue.
3. **Offer a Solution**: In your response, provide a solution or offer to address the customer's concerns. This could involve offering a refund, replacement, or any other appropriate resolution. Be clear and transparent about what you can do to rectify the situation.
4. **Take the Conversation Offline**: If the issue requires further discussion or resolution, it is best to take the conversation offline. Provide the customer with a contact method, such as an email address or phone number, where they can reach you directly. This allows for a more personalized and private conversation.

Remember, negative reviews can also provide an opportunity for growth and improvement. Use them as a learning experience to enhance your products or services and demonstrate your commitment to customer satisfaction.

5.2.4 Responding to Neutral or Mixed Reviews

Not all reviews fall into the category of strictly positive or negative. Etsy recognizes that some reviews may be neutral or mixed, and provides guidance on how to respond:

1. **Express Appreciation**: Regardless of the tone or content of the review, always express appreciation for the customer's feedback. Let them know that their opinion is valued and that you take their comments seriously.
2. **Address Specific Concerns**: If the review mentions specific concerns or issues, address them directly in your response. Provide any necessary clarification or information to help the customer understand your perspective.
3. **Offer Assistance**: Even if the review is not overwhelmingly positive, offer assistance or support to the customer. Let them know that you are available to address any further questions or concerns they may have.

By responding to neutral or mixed reviews in a thoughtful and helpful manner, you can demonstrate your commitment to customer satisfaction and potentially turn a neutral experience into a positive one.

Understanding Etsy's review policies is essential for effectively responding to customer reviews on the platform. By adhering to these policies and guidelines, you can maintain a positive reputation, build trust with customers, and enhance your overall business success on Etsy.

5.3 Addressing Business-Specific Review Challenges

As a business owner on Etsy, you may encounter specific challenges when it comes to addressing reviews. Each business is unique, and understanding how to navigate these challenges can help you craft effective responses that resonate with your customers. In this section, we will explore some common business-specific review challenges and provide strategies for addressing them.

5.3.1 Managing Custom Orders and Personalization

One of the unique aspects of running a business on Etsy is the ability to offer custom orders and personalized products. While this can be a great selling point, it can also present challenges when it comes to reviews. Customers may have specific expectations or preferences for their custom orders, and it's important to address any concerns or issues they may have.

When responding to reviews for custom orders, it's essential to acknowledge the customer's unique requirements and demonstrate your commitment to providing a personalized experience. Start by thanking the customer for their feedback and expressing your appreciation for their support. Then, address any specific concerns they may have raised in their review.

If there was a mistake or misunderstanding with the customization process, apologize and offer a solution to rectify the situation. This could involve offering a replacement or refund, or working closely with the customer to find a resolution that meets their needs. By showing empathy and a willingness to make things right, you can turn a potentially negative review into a positive customer experience.

5.3.2 Handling Shipping and Delivery Issues

Shipping and delivery issues are common challenges for businesses on Etsy, especially for those selling physical products. Delays, lost packages, or damaged items can lead to negative reviews and customer dissatisfaction. It's crucial to address these concerns promptly and effectively to maintain a positive reputation.

When responding to reviews about shipping and delivery issues, start by expressing your understanding of the customer's frustration. Apologize for any inconvenience caused and assure them that you take their concerns seriously. Provide a clear explanation of the situation, whether it was due to unforeseen circumstances or a mistake on your end.

Offer a solution to resolve the issue, such as providing a replacement or refund, or working with the customer to track down a lost package. If the issue was beyond your control, such as a delay caused by the shipping carrier, communicate this to the customer and provide any relevant tracking information or documentation.

By taking ownership of the problem and offering a solution, you can demonstrate your commitment to customer satisfaction and turn a negative experience into a positive one.

5.3.3 Managing Inventory and Product Availability

Another challenge that Etsy businesses may face is managing inventory and product availability. It can be disappointing for customers to discover that an item they wanted to purchase is out of stock or no longer available. Addressing these concerns in your responses is crucial to maintaining customer trust and loyalty.

When responding to reviews about inventory and product availability, start by expressing your regret for any inconvenience caused. Apologize for the disappointment and explain the reasons behind the unavailability, whether it's due to high demand, limited supplies, or a temporary issue.

Offer alternative options or suggestions to the customer, such as similar products or upcoming restocks. If possible, provide a timeline for when the item will be back in stock or offer to notify the customer when it becomes available again. By showing proactive communication and a willingness to assist, you can mitigate any negative impact on the customer's experience.

5.3.4 Addressing Pricing and Value Concerns

Pricing and value concerns can arise when customers feel that the product they received does not meet their expectations or justify the price they paid. It's important to address these concerns in a thoughtful and understanding manner to maintain customer satisfaction.

When responding to reviews about pricing and value concerns, start by acknowledging the customer's feedback and expressing your appreciation for their input. Avoid becoming defensive or dismissive of their concerns. Instead, focus on providing a clear explanation of the value and quality of your products.

Highlight any unique features, materials, or craftsmanship that set your products apart. If applicable, provide examples or testimonials from satisfied customers who have found value in your offerings. Offer to address any specific issues the customer may have encountered, such as providing a replacement or refund if the product did not meet their expectations.

By addressing pricing and value concerns with transparency and empathy, you can demonstrate your commitment to customer satisfaction and potentially turn a negative review into a positive one.

5.3.5 Dealing with Communication Challenges

Effective communication is essential for any business, and Etsy is no exception. However, communication challenges can arise, such as delays in responding to messages or misunderstandings in product descriptions. Addressing these challenges in your review responses is crucial to maintaining customer trust and satisfaction.

When responding to reviews about communication challenges, start by apologizing for any inconvenience caused by the lack of communication or misunderstanding. Take responsibility for any shortcomings and assure the customer that you value their feedback.

Explain any reasons behind the communication challenges, such as high volume or technical issues. Offer a solution to address the customer's concerns, such as improving response times or clarifying product descriptions. If necessary, provide alternative contact methods or channels for better communication in the future.

By demonstrating your commitment to improving communication and addressing any concerns, you can rebuild trust with the customer and enhance their overall experience.

Remember, addressing business-specific review challenges requires empathy, understanding, and a commitment to customer satisfaction. By implementing the strategies outlined in this section, you can effectively navigate these challenges and craft responses that resonate with your customers on Etsy.

5.4 Tips for Responding to Etsy Reviews

Responding to Etsy reviews is an essential part of managing your online reputation and building a strong relationship with your customers. Whether the review is positive, negative, or neutral, your response can make a significant impact on how your business is perceived. In this section, we will provide you with some valuable tips for crafting effective responses to Etsy reviews.

5.4.1 Show Appreciation and Gratitude

When responding to positive Etsy reviews, it is crucial to express your appreciation and gratitude to the customer. Start by thanking them for taking the time to leave a review and for their kind words. Let them know that their feedback means a lot to you and your business. Showing genuine appreciation will not only make the customer feel valued but also encourage others to leave positive reviews.

Example response: "Thank you so much for your kind words! We truly appreciate you taking the time to leave a review. Your support means the world to us, and we're thrilled to hear that you had a great experience with our product. We look forward to serving you again in the future!"

5.4.2 Personalize Your Responses

Make your responses to Etsy reviews personal and authentic. Address the customer by their name if it is provided, and use a friendly and conversational tone. Personalization shows that you value each customer as an individual and not just another sale. It also helps to create a connection and build trust with your customers.

Example response: "Hi [Customer's Name], thank you for your wonderful review! We're thrilled to hear that you loved our product. It means a lot to us that you took the time to share your experience. We hope to see you again soon!"

5.4.3 Address Specific Points

When responding to Etsy reviews, take the time to address any specific points or compliments mentioned by the customer. This shows that you have read and understood their review and that you genuinely care about their feedback. By addressing specific points, you also provide potential customers with more information about your product or service.

Example response: "Thank you for your kind words about our customer service! We strive to provide the best support possible, and we're glad to hear that it made a difference for you. If you have any further questions or need assistance in the future, please don't hesitate to reach out. We're here to help!"

5.4.4 Apologize and Offer Solutions for Negative Reviews

When responding to negative Etsy reviews, it is essential to remain calm and professional. Start by apologizing for the customer's negative experience and acknowledge their concerns. Avoid getting defensive or making excuses. Instead, offer a solution or ask the customer to contact you privately to resolve the issue. This shows that you are committed to resolving problems and providing excellent customer service.

Example response: "We're sorry to hear about your negative experience with our product. That's not the level of quality we strive for, and we apologize for any inconvenience caused. We would like to make it right for you. Please reach out to us privately, and we'll do our best to resolve the issue to your satisfaction."

5.4.5 Respond Promptly

Timely responses to Etsy reviews are crucial for maintaining a positive image for your business. Aim to respond to reviews within 24-48 hours, if possible. Prompt responses show that you are actively engaged with your customers and care about their feedback. It also demonstrates your commitment to providing excellent customer service.

Example response: "Thank you for your review! We appreciate your feedback and are thrilled to hear that you had a positive experience with our product. If you have any further questions or need assistance, please don't hesitate to reach out. We're here to help!"

5.4.6 Monitor and Learn from Reviews

Regularly monitor your Etsy reviews to stay informed about customer feedback and identify areas for improvement. Pay attention to recurring themes or issues mentioned in negative reviews and use them as an opportunity to make necessary changes to your products or services. Learning from reviews can help you enhance customer satisfaction and ultimately improve your business.

Example response: "Thank you for your feedback. We apologize for any inconvenience caused and appreciate you bringing this to our attention. We take customer feedback seriously, and we'll use it to improve our products and services. If there's anything else we can do to assist you, please let us know."

Remember, responding to Etsy reviews is not only about addressing individual customers but also about showcasing your commitment to excellent customer service to potential buyers. By following these tips and crafting thoughtful responses, you can build a positive reputation, strengthen customer relationships, and ultimately drive more sales for your Etsy business.

6 Prompts and Answers Bank

6.1 Creating a Bank of Review Prompts

One of the most effective ways to craft authentic and personalized responses to positive reviews is by creating a bank of review prompts. These prompts can serve as a starting point for your responses, helping you to provide thoughtful and meaningful replies to your customers. In this section, we will explore how to create a bank of review prompts and provide examples of prompts that you can use for your own business.

6.1.1 Understanding the Importance of Review Prompts

Review prompts are pre-written statements or questions that can guide your response to a positive review. They help you to structure your response and ensure that you address the key points mentioned by the customer. By using review prompts, you can save time and effort while still providing a personalized and genuine response.

Review prompts are particularly useful for businesses that receive a high volume of positive reviews. It can be challenging to come up with unique and engaging responses for each review, especially when you have limited time. Having a bank of review prompts allows you to streamline the process and respond to reviews efficiently, without sacrificing the personal touch.

6.1.2 Creating Your Bank of Review Prompts

To create your bank of review prompts, start by analyzing the common themes and sentiments expressed in your positive reviews. Look for recurring compliments, specific aspects of your product or service that customers appreciate, and any unique experiences mentioned by your customers. These insights will help you identify the key areas to focus on when crafting your review prompts.

Once you have identified the themes, create a list of prompts that can be used as a starting point for your responses. Each prompt should be tailored to address a specific aspect of the customer's review. For example, if customers frequently mention the exceptional customer service they received, you can create a prompt like:

- "Thank you for your kind words about our customer service! We strive to provide the best experience for our customers, and we're thrilled to hear that we exceeded your expectations. It was a pleasure serving you, and we look forward to assisting you in the future."

Remember to keep your prompts concise and genuine. Avoid using generic or robotic-sounding language. The goal is to create prompts that feel personal and authentic to your brand.

6.1.3 Examples of Review Prompts

To give you a better idea of how review prompts can be used, here are some examples that you can adapt for your own business:

1. "We're delighted to hear that you love our product! It was designed with [specific feature] in mind, and we're thrilled that it met your expectations. Thank you for your support!"
2. "Thank you for your kind words about our team! We take pride in providing excellent customer service, and we're glad that it made a difference in your experience. We appreciate your feedback!"
3. "We're so happy to hear that our product has made a positive impact in your life. Your satisfaction is our top

priority, and we're grateful for your support. If you have any further questions or need assistance, please don't hesitate to reach out."

4. "We're thrilled that our service exceeded your expectations! Our team works hard to ensure that every customer has a memorable experience. Thank you for choosing us, and we look forward to serving you again in the future."

5. "We're grateful for your kind words about our packaging. We believe that presentation is an important part of the overall experience, and we're glad it made a difference for you. Thank you for your support!"

Remember, these prompts are just a starting point. Feel free to customize them to fit your brand's tone and voice. The key is to use them as a guide to help you craft personalized responses that resonate with your customers.

6.1.4 Using Your Bank of Review Prompts

Once you have created your bank of review prompts, it's time to put them into action. When responding to positive reviews, refer to your prompts and select the one that best aligns with the customer's feedback. Use the prompt as a foundation for your response and add any additional personalization or details as needed.

While using review prompts can save time, it's important to remember that each response should still feel genuine and sincere. Take the time to read and understand the customer's review before selecting a prompt and crafting your response. This will ensure that your reply is relevant and meaningful to the customer.

By creating a bank of review prompts, you can streamline the process of responding to positive reviews while still providing personalized and authentic responses. Use these prompts as a starting point, and customize them to fit your brand's voice and style. Your customers will appreciate the thoughtful and genuine replies, and it will help to strengthen your relationship with them.

6.2 Crafting Authentic and Personalized Responses

Crafting authentic and personalized responses to reviews is crucial for building strong relationships with your customers and showcasing your commitment to their satisfaction. In this section, we will explore the importance of authenticity in your responses and provide you with practical tips on how to personalize your replies to create a meaningful connection with your customers.

6.2.1 The Power of Authenticity

Authenticity is the key to establishing trust and credibility with your customers. When responding to reviews, it is essential to convey a genuine and sincere tone that reflects your appreciation for their feedback. Authentic responses show that you value your customers' opinions and are committed to providing exceptional service.

To craft authentic responses, consider the following tips:

1. Use the reviewer's name: Addressing the reviewer by their name adds a personal touch to your response and shows that you have taken the time to acknowledge them individually.

2. Express gratitude: Begin your response by expressing your gratitude for the customer's positive review. Let them know that their feedback is valuable to you and that you appreciate their support.

3. Be specific: Highlight specific aspects of the customer's experience that they mentioned in their review. This shows that you have read their feedback carefully and are genuinely interested in their satisfaction.

4. Use a conversational tone: Write your response in a friendly and conversational tone. Avoid using overly formal language or generic phrases. Instead, aim for a warm and approachable style that resonates with your

brand's personality.

5. Offer a personal touch: Whenever possible, include personalized details in your response. For example, if the customer mentioned a specific product or service they enjoyed, acknowledge it and express your delight in their satisfaction.

6. Avoid generic responses: While it may be tempting to use pre-written templates, try to avoid generic responses. Customers appreciate personalized replies that address their specific feedback. Take the time to craft a unique response for each review.

6.2.2 Tailoring Responses to Different Review Types

Different types of reviews require different approaches when crafting your responses. Let's explore how to tailor your replies to various review scenarios:

Positive Reviews

When responding to positive reviews, your goal is to reinforce the customer's positive experience and express your gratitude. Here are some tips for crafting responses to positive reviews:

1. Express appreciation: Begin by thanking the customer for their positive feedback. Let them know that their satisfaction is your top priority.

2. Highlight specific positive aspects: Identify specific elements of the customer's experience that they mentioned in their review. Emphasize these positive aspects and show that you value their feedback.

3. Encourage future engagement: Invite the customer to continue their relationship with your business. For example, you can suggest they explore other products or services you offer or invite them to follow your social media accounts for updates and promotions.

4. Offer a discount or special offer: As a token of appreciation, consider offering a discount or special offer to customers who leave positive reviews. This gesture can encourage repeat business and further strengthen the customer's loyalty.

Negative Reviews

Responding to negative reviews requires a delicate approach. Your goal is to address the customer's concerns, provide a solution, and demonstrate your commitment to resolving the issue. Here are some tips for crafting responses to negative reviews:

1. Apologize and acknowledge the issue: Begin by expressing your sincere apologies for the customer's negative experience. Let them know that their feedback is valuable, and you take their concerns seriously.

2. Offer a solution: Provide a clear and actionable solution to the customer's problem. Offer to rectify the issue, whether it's through a refund, replacement, or any other appropriate resolution.

3. Take the conversation offline: If the issue requires further discussion or sensitive information, encourage the customer to contact you privately. Provide them with your contact details or direct them to a customer support channel where they can address their concerns.

4. Show empathy and understanding: Demonstrate empathy towards the customer's frustration or disappointment. Let them know that you understand their perspective and are committed to improving their experience.

Neutral or Mixed Reviews

Responding to neutral or mixed reviews requires a balanced approach. Your goal is to address any concerns raised by the customer while also highlighting positive aspects of their feedback. Here are some tips for crafting responses to neutral or mixed reviews:

1. Thank the customer for their feedback: Begin by expressing your appreciation for the customer's review. Let them know that you value their input and are committed to addressing their concerns.
2. Address specific concerns: Identify any specific concerns or issues raised by the customer and provide a thoughtful response. Offer solutions or explanations where appropriate.
3. Highlight positive aspects: Identify any positive aspects mentioned in the review and acknowledge them. Emphasize that you value the customer's feedback and are continuously working to improve their experience.
4. Offer assistance: Extend an offer to assist the customer further if they require additional support or have any unresolved issues. Provide them with contact information or direct them to the appropriate customer support channels.

6.2.3 Adding a Personal Touch

Adding a personal touch to your responses can make a significant impact on your customers. Here are some additional tips for personalizing your replies:

1. Use the customer's name: Address the customer by their name to create a more personal connection. This simple gesture shows that you value them as an individual.
2. Reference previous interactions: If the customer has had previous interactions with your business, reference those interactions in your response. This demonstrates that you remember them and their history with your brand.
3. Share relevant information: If you have any relevant information or updates to share with the customer, include it in your response. This could be upcoming promotions, new product releases, or any other information that may be of interest to them.
4. Sign off with a personal touch: Instead of using a generic closing, consider signing off with a personalized message. This could be a simple "Best regards" followed by your name or a more personalized closing that aligns with your brand's tone and personality.

By following these tips and tailoring your responses to different review types, you can create authentic and personalized replies that resonate with your customers. Remember, each response is an opportunity to strengthen your relationship with your customers and showcase your commitment to their satisfaction.

6.3 Commonly Asked Questions and Answers

In this section, we will address some commonly asked questions about crafting effective responses to positive reviews, as well as provide you with a bank of prompts and answers specifically tailored for Etsy and business-related reviews. We will also discuss how to handle feedback and provide answers to common feedback-related questions.

6.3.1 How should I respond to a positive review?

When responding to a positive review, it's important to show gratitude and appreciation for the customer's feedback. Here is an example response:

"Thank you so much for your kind words! We are thrilled to hear that you had a positive experience with our product/service. Your satisfaction is our top priority, and we are grateful for your support. If you have any further questions or need assistance in the future, please don't hesitate to reach out. Thank you again for choosing our business!"

Remember to keep your response personalized and authentic. Use the customer's name if possible and mention specific details from their review to show that you have read and appreciated their feedback.

6.3.2 How can I leverage positive reviews to promote my business?

Positive reviews are a powerful marketing tool. Here are a few ways you can leverage them to promote your business:

1. Share positive reviews on your website or social media platforms to showcase customer satisfaction and build trust with potential customers.
2. Use snippets from positive reviews in your marketing materials, such as email newsletters or advertisements.
3. Encourage satisfied customers to leave reviews on other platforms, such as Google or Yelp, to expand your online presence and reputation.
4. Consider offering incentives, such as discounts or rewards, to customers who leave positive reviews to encourage more feedback.

6.3.3 How can I handle feedback effectively?

Handling feedback effectively is crucial for continuous improvement and customer satisfaction. Here are some tips:

1. Listen attentively: Take the time to understand the customer's concerns or suggestions.
2. Respond promptly: Address feedback in a timely manner to show that you value the customer's input.
3. Apologize if necessary: If the feedback highlights a valid issue or problem, apologize sincerely and offer a solution.
4. Take action: Use feedback to make improvements to your products or services.
5. Follow up: Reach out to the customer after implementing changes to show that their feedback was taken seriously.

6.3.4 How can I use feedback to improve my products and services?

Feedback is a valuable source of information for improving your products and services. Here are some ways you can utilize feedback effectively:

1. Identify patterns: Look for common themes or issues mentioned in multiple feedbacks to identify areas for improvement.
2. Prioritize changes: Determine which feedback requires immediate attention and focus on making necessary changes.
3. Involve your team: Share feedback with your team and encourage brainstorming sessions to come up with innovative solutions.
4. Test and iterate: Implement changes based on feedback and monitor the impact. Continuously iterate and improve based on customer input.

6.3.5 How can I encourage customers to provide feedback?

Encouraging customers to provide feedback is essential for gathering valuable insights. Here are some strategies to encourage feedback:

1. Ask for feedback directly: Include a personalized note or email asking customers to share their experience and provide feedback.
2. Offer incentives: Consider offering discounts, freebies, or loyalty rewards to customers who leave feedback.
3. Make it easy: Provide clear instructions on how to leave feedback and ensure the process is simple and user-friendly.
4. Follow up: Reach out to customers after their purchase to ask for feedback and show that you value their opinion.

6.3.6 How can I use the Etsy platform to maximize positive reviews?

Etsy provides a unique platform for sellers to showcase their products and receive reviews. Here are some tips for maximizing positive reviews on Etsy:

1. Provide excellent customer service: Respond promptly to inquiries, offer personalized assistance, and go the extra mile to exceed customer expectations.
2. Offer high-quality products: Ensure that your products meet or exceed the expectations set in your listings.
3. Encourage reviews: Include a note in your packaging or follow-up email asking customers to leave a review if they are satisfied with their purchase.
4. Engage with the Etsy community: Participate in forums, join teams, and support other sellers to build a positive reputation within the Etsy community.

Remember, positive reviews are a reflection of your hard work and dedication to customer satisfaction. Utilize them to build trust, promote your business, and continuously improve your products and services.

6.4 Using the Bank for Efficient Responses

In the previous sections, we discussed the importance of crafting effective responses to reviews and provided you with a bank of review prompts and commonly asked questions. Now, let's explore how you can use this bank to efficiently respond to reviews, specifically focusing on positive reviews, Etsy reviews, and feedback.

6.4.1 Efficiently Responding to Positive Reviews

Positive reviews are a great opportunity to engage with your customers and show your appreciation for their support. By using the bank of review prompts, you can quickly and efficiently respond to these reviews while still providing a personalized touch. Here are some examples of how you can use the bank for efficient responses to positive reviews:

1. **Thanking the customer**: Start by expressing your gratitude for the positive review. You can use prompts like:

   - "Thank you so much for your kind words!"
   - "We're thrilled to hear that you had a great experience with us!"
   - "We appreciate your support and feedback!"

1. **Highlighting specific aspects**: If the customer mentioned specific aspects of their experience, acknowledge and appreciate them. Use prompts such as:

– "We're glad you loved our product/service. Our team works hard to ensure the highest quality."

– "It's great to hear that our customer service exceeded your expectations. We strive to provide excellent support to all our customers."

1. **Encouraging future engagement**: Use prompts to encourage the customer to continue their relationship with your business:

– "We look forward to serving you again in the future!"

– "Don't hesitate to reach out if you have any more questions or need further assistance."

By using the bank of review prompts, you can quickly and efficiently respond to positive reviews, ensuring that each response is personalized and appreciative.

6.4.2 Efficiently Responding to Etsy Reviews

As an Etsy seller, responding to reviews is crucial for building trust and credibility with your customers. The bank of review prompts can be a valuable resource in efficiently responding to Etsy reviews. Here are some examples of how you can use the bank for efficient responses to Etsy reviews:

1. **Acknowledging the purchase**: Start by acknowledging the customer's purchase and expressing your appreciation. You can use prompts like:

– "Thank you for choosing our shop for your purchase!"

– "We're grateful that you chose our product among the many options on Etsy."

1. **Addressing specific product details**: If the customer mentioned specific details about the product, acknowledge and address them. Use prompts such as:

– "We're glad you liked the color/size/design of the product. We put a lot of effort into ensuring the highest quality."

– "It's great to hear that the product arrived in perfect condition. We take extra care in packaging to prevent any damage during shipping."

1. **Offering assistance**: Use prompts to offer further assistance or support to the customer:

– "If you have any questions or need any further assistance, please don't hesitate to reach out to us."

– "We're here to help, so feel free to contact us if you need anything."

By utilizing the bank of review prompts, you can efficiently respond to Etsy reviews, demonstrating your commitment to customer satisfaction and building a positive reputation on the platform.

6.4.3 Efficiently Responding to Feedback

Feedback is a valuable source of information for improving your products and services. By using the bank of review prompts, you can efficiently respond to feedback and address any concerns or suggestions. Here are some examples of how you can use the bank for efficient responses to feedback:

1. **Acknowledging the feedback**: Start by acknowledging the customer's feedback and expressing your appreciation for their input. You can use prompts like:

– "Thank you for taking the time to provide us with your feedback. We value your opinion."

– "We appreciate your feedback and will take it into consideration as we continue to improve."

1. **Addressing concerns or issues**: If the feedback includes specific concerns or issues, address them directly and offer a solution. Use prompts such as:

– "We apologize for any inconvenience you experienced. Please contact our customer support team, and we will resolve the issue promptly."

– "Thank you for bringing this to our attention. We will investigate the matter and take the necessary steps to prevent it from happening again."

1. **Explaining improvements**: If the feedback suggests areas for improvement, explain the steps you are taking to address those concerns. Use prompts such as:

– "We are constantly working to improve our products/services, and your feedback helps us in that process. We have taken note of your suggestions and will implement them in our future updates."

By utilizing the bank of review prompts, you can efficiently respond to feedback, showing your customers that their opinions are valued and that you are committed to continuous improvement.

In conclusion, the bank of review prompts and commonly asked questions can be powerful tools for efficiently responding to positive reviews, Etsy reviews, and feedback. By using these resources, you can save time while still providing personalized and meaningful responses to your customers. Remember, efficient responses not only show your appreciation but also contribute to building a positive reputation and fostering customer loyalty.

7 Maximizing the Benefits of Stellar Reviews

7.1 Leveraging Reviews for Marketing and Branding

Reviews are not just a way for customers to share their experiences with a product or service; they can also be a powerful tool for marketing and branding. When used effectively, reviews can help businesses build trust, credibility, and loyalty among their target audience. In this section, we will explore how you can leverage reviews to enhance your marketing and branding efforts.

7.1.1 Showcasing Social Proof

One of the most significant benefits of positive reviews is the social proof they provide. When potential customers see positive feedback from others who have already purchased and enjoyed your product or service, it can significantly influence their decision-making process. By leveraging these reviews, you can showcase social proof and build trust with your target audience.

To maximize the impact of positive reviews on your marketing and branding, consider the following strategies:

1. **Feature reviews on your website**: Displaying positive reviews prominently on your website can help potential customers see the value and quality of your offerings. Consider creating a dedicated section or a testimonial page where you can showcase these reviews.
2. **Include reviews in your marketing materials**: Incorporate snippets of positive reviews in your marketing materials, such as brochures, flyers, or social media posts. By including these testimonials, you can provide potential customers with real-life examples of satisfied customers.
3. **Utilize reviews in your advertising campaigns**: When running online or offline advertising campaigns, consider incorporating positive reviews into your ad copy. This can help capture the attention of potential customers and increase their interest in your product or service.
4. **Leverage reviews in your email marketing**: Include snippets of positive reviews in your email newsletters or promotional emails. This can help reinforce the trust and credibility of your brand and encourage recipients to take action.

7.1.2 Engaging with Customers

Reviews provide an excellent opportunity for businesses to engage with their customers and build a strong relationship. By actively responding to reviews, you can show your customers that you value their feedback and are committed to providing exceptional customer service. This engagement can have a positive impact on your marketing and branding efforts.

Consider the following strategies to engage with customers through reviews:

1. **Respond to all reviews**: Whether the review is positive, negative, or neutral, make it a practice to respond to every review. Thank customers for their positive feedback, address any concerns raised in negative reviews, and express your willingness to resolve any issues.
2. **Personalize your responses**: Avoid generic or automated responses. Take the time to craft personalized responses that acknowledge the specific feedback provided by the customer. This shows that you genuinely care about their experience and are committed to addressing their needs.
3. **Highlight customer feedback in your responses**: When responding to positive reviews, highlight specific

aspects of the customer's experience that they appreciated. This not only shows your gratitude but also reinforces the positive aspects of your product or service.

4. **Offer solutions and assistance**: In your responses to negative reviews, demonstrate your commitment to resolving any issues. Offer solutions, apologize for any inconvenience caused, and provide contact information for further assistance. This shows potential customers that you are proactive in addressing concerns and providing excellent customer service.

7.1.3 Leveraging Reviews in Social Media

Social media platforms provide an excellent opportunity to leverage reviews for marketing and branding purposes. With millions of active users, social media platforms allow you to reach a wide audience and engage with potential customers directly. Here are some strategies to leverage reviews on social media:

1. **Share positive reviews on social media**: Take screenshots or snippets of positive reviews and share them on your social media profiles. This can help increase brand visibility and attract new customers who may be interested in your product or service.
2. **Encourage customers to share their reviews on social media**: Include a call-to-action in your responses to positive reviews, encouraging customers to share their experience on social media. This can help generate user-generated content and increase brand awareness among their followers.
3. **Engage with customers on social media**: Monitor your social media profiles for reviews and engage with customers by responding to their comments or messages. This shows that you are actively listening to their feedback and are committed to providing excellent customer service.
4. **Run social media contests or giveaways**: Encourage customers to leave reviews by running contests or giveaways on social media. Offer incentives such as discounts, freebies, or exclusive access to new products or services. This can help generate a buzz around your brand and encourage customers to share their positive experiences.

By leveraging reviews for marketing and branding, you can tap into the power of social proof, engage with customers, and increase brand visibility. Remember to always respond to reviews promptly and professionally, and use the feedback to continuously improve your products and services.

7.2 Building Trust and Credibility with Reviews

Building trust and credibility with reviews is essential for the success of any business. Positive reviews not only serve as a testament to the quality of your products or services but also help establish your brand's reputation. In this section, we will explore strategies to build trust and credibility through reviews.

7.2.1 Encourage Authentic and Genuine Reviews

One of the most effective ways to build trust and credibility with reviews is by encouraging authentic and genuine feedback from your customers. When customers see that your reviews are genuine and not manipulated, they are more likely to trust the opinions and experiences shared by others.

To encourage authentic reviews, make it easy for customers to leave feedback. Provide clear instructions on how to leave a review and consider offering incentives such as discounts or rewards for leaving a review. However, it is important to note that incentivizing reviews should be done ethically and within the guidelines of the platform you are using.

7.2.2 Respond Promptly and Professionally

Responding promptly and professionally to reviews is another crucial aspect of building trust and credibility. When customers see that you are actively engaged and responsive to their feedback, it shows that you value their opinions and are committed to providing excellent customer service.

Ensure that you have a system in place to monitor and respond to reviews in a timely manner. Acknowledge positive reviews with gratitude and address any concerns or issues raised in negative reviews with empathy and a willingness to resolve the problem. By demonstrating your commitment to customer satisfaction, you can build trust and credibility with both existing and potential customers.

7.2.3 Showcase Positive Reviews on Your Website or Social Media

Another effective way to build trust and credibility with reviews is by showcasing positive reviews on your website or social media platforms. This allows potential customers to see the positive experiences others have had with your business, further reinforcing their trust in your brand.

Consider creating a dedicated section on your website to highlight positive reviews. You can also share snippets of positive reviews on your social media channels, along with a link to the full review. By sharing these testimonials, you are providing social proof of your business's credibility and encouraging others to trust and engage with your brand.

7.2.4 Engage with Reviewers and Address Concerns

Engaging with reviewers and addressing their concerns is a crucial step in building trust and credibility. When customers see that you are actively listening and taking their feedback seriously, it enhances their trust in your brand.

Respond to both positive and negative reviews in a respectful and empathetic manner. Thank customers for their positive feedback and address any specific points they mentioned. For negative reviews, acknowledge the customer's concerns, apologize if necessary, and offer a solution or resolution to the problem. By demonstrating your commitment to customer satisfaction, you can turn a negative experience into a positive one and build trust with your customers.

7.2.5 Monitor and Manage Your Online Reputation

Monitoring and managing your online reputation is vital for building trust and credibility with reviews. Regularly check review platforms, social media channels, and other online sources for feedback about your business. Respond promptly to reviews and address any issues or concerns raised.

In addition to responding to individual reviews, it is important to monitor and analyze review trends. Look for common themes or patterns in the feedback you receive. This can provide valuable insights into areas where you can improve your products or services, further enhancing your credibility and trustworthiness.

7.2.6 Leverage Influencer and Celebrity Endorsements

Influencer and celebrity endorsements can significantly boost your brand's trust and credibility. When influential individuals or celebrities endorse your products or services, it adds a level of credibility and trustworthiness that can be difficult to achieve through other means.

Consider reaching out to relevant influencers or celebrities in your industry and offering them your products or services for review. If they have a positive experience, they may be willing to share their feedback with their followers, further enhancing your brand's reputation.

However, it is important to ensure that any endorsements are genuine and align with your brand values. Transparency is key, and customers appreciate authenticity in endorsements.

7.2.7 Implement Feedback and Improve Your Products or Services

One of the most powerful ways to build trust and credibility with reviews is by implementing feedback and continuously improving your products or services. When customers see that their feedback is taken into account and results in tangible improvements, it enhances their trust in your brand.

Regularly review the feedback you receive and identify areas where you can make enhancements or address concerns. This could involve making changes to your products, improving customer service processes, or refining your overall business strategy. By actively seeking feedback and implementing changes based on customer input, you demonstrate your commitment to providing the best possible experience, which in turn builds trust and credibility.

In conclusion, building trust and credibility with reviews is crucial for the success of your business. Encourage authentic and genuine reviews, respond promptly and professionally, showcase positive reviews, engage with reviewers, monitor and manage your online reputation, leverage influencer and celebrity endorsements, and implement feedback to continuously improve your products or services. By following these strategies, you can establish a strong reputation and build trust with your customers, ultimately leading to business growth and success.

7.3 Using Reviews to Improve Products and Services

Customer reviews are not only valuable for marketing and building trust, but they can also provide valuable insights into how you can improve your products and services. By carefully analyzing and understanding the feedback provided in reviews, you can identify areas of improvement and make necessary changes to enhance the overall customer experience. In this section, we will explore how you can effectively use reviews to improve your products and services.

7.3.1 Analyzing Review Feedback

To begin using reviews to improve your products and services, it is essential to analyze the feedback provided by customers. Start by categorizing the reviews based on common themes or concerns. Look for patterns in the feedback to identify recurring issues or areas where customers are particularly satisfied. This analysis will help you prioritize the improvements that need to be made.

7.3.2 Identifying Areas for Improvement

Once you have analyzed the review feedback, it's time to identify specific areas for improvement. Pay attention to both positive and negative reviews, as they can provide valuable insights. Positive reviews can highlight aspects of your products or services that customers appreciate, while negative reviews can point out areas that need attention.

Consider the following questions when identifying areas for improvement:

1. Are there any recurring complaints or concerns mentioned in the negative reviews?
2. Are there any suggestions or recommendations provided by customers in their reviews?
3. Are there any features or aspects of your products or services that consistently receive positive feedback?
4. Are there any common themes or patterns in the reviews that indicate areas for improvement?

By answering these questions, you can pinpoint specific areas that require your attention and focus your efforts on making necessary improvements.

7.3.3 Implementing Changes Based on Review Feedback

Once you have identified the areas for improvement, it's time to implement the necessary changes. Consider the following steps to effectively incorporate review feedback into your product or service enhancements:

1. Prioritize the changes: Start by prioritizing the identified areas for improvement based on their impact on the overall customer experience. Focus on addressing the most critical issues first.
2. Develop an action plan: Create a detailed action plan outlining the steps you need to take to address each area for improvement. Assign responsibilities to team members and set realistic timelines for implementing the changes.
3. Communicate with your team: Share the review feedback and the action plan with your team members. Ensure everyone understands the importance of the changes and their role in implementing them.
4. Make necessary adjustments: Based on the review feedback, make the necessary adjustments to your products or services. This may involve modifying features, improving customer service processes, or enhancing the overall user experience.
5. Test and iterate: After implementing the changes, monitor the impact on customer satisfaction and gather feedback from customers. Use this feedback to further refine and iterate on your improvements.

7.3.4 Encouraging Customer Feedback for Continuous Improvement

To continuously improve your products and services, it is crucial to encourage ongoing customer feedback. Here are some strategies to encourage customers to provide feedback:

1. Request reviews: After a customer makes a purchase or uses your service, send them a follow-up email requesting their feedback. Make it easy for them to leave a review by providing clear instructions and links to review platforms.
2. Offer incentives: Consider offering incentives such as discounts, exclusive offers, or loyalty rewards to customers who provide feedback. This can motivate them to share their thoughts and experiences.
3. Create a feedback form: Develop a simple and user-friendly feedback form on your website or within your app. Ask specific questions about their experience and provide an open-ended section for additional comments.
4. Engage on social media: Monitor social media platforms for mentions of your brand or products. Respond to customer comments and encourage them to share their feedback openly.
5. Conduct surveys: Periodically conduct surveys to gather more detailed feedback from your customers. Offer incentives for completing the survey to increase participation.

By actively seeking and encouraging customer feedback, you can gather valuable insights that will help you make informed decisions and continuously improve your products and services.

7.3.5 Monitoring the Impact of Changes on Reviews

After implementing changes based on review feedback, it is essential to monitor the impact of these changes on customer reviews. Regularly check review platforms and analyze the new feedback received. Look for trends and patterns in the reviews to assess whether the changes have had a positive impact on customer satisfaction.

If you notice improvements in the reviews, it indicates that your efforts to address customer concerns have been successful. However, if negative feedback persists or new issues arise, it may be necessary to revisit your action plan and make further adjustments.

Remember, the process of using reviews to improve your products and services is an ongoing one. Continuously monitor and analyze customer feedback, make necessary changes, and strive for continuous improvement to ensure customer satisfaction and business success.

By leveraging the power of customer reviews, you can gain valuable insights into how to enhance your products and services, ultimately leading to increased customer satisfaction and loyalty.

7.4 Monitoring and Analyzing Review Trends

Monitoring and analyzing review trends is a crucial aspect of managing your online reputation and understanding the sentiment of your customers. By keeping a close eye on the reviews you receive, you can gain valuable insights into the strengths and weaknesses of your business, identify areas for improvement, and make informed decisions to enhance customer satisfaction. In this section, we will explore the importance of monitoring and analyzing review trends and provide you with practical tips on how to do it effectively.

7.4.1 The Importance of Monitoring Review Trends

Monitoring review trends allows you to stay informed about what customers are saying about your business. It provides you with a pulse on customer satisfaction and helps you identify patterns and trends in the feedback you receive. Here are a few reasons why monitoring review trends is essential:

1. Identifying areas for improvement:

By analyzing the common themes and concerns raised in negative or mixed reviews, you can pinpoint areas of your business that may need attention. Whether it's a specific product issue, customer service problem, or shipping delay, monitoring review trends helps you identify patterns and take proactive steps to address them.

2. Tracking the impact of changes:

If you have recently implemented changes based on customer feedback, monitoring review trends allows you to assess the effectiveness of those changes. By comparing the sentiment and content of reviews before and after the implementation, you can gauge whether your efforts have had a positive impact on customer satisfaction.

3. Spotting emerging trends:

Review trends can provide valuable insights into emerging trends in customer preferences or expectations. By staying ahead of these trends, you can adapt your products, services, or policies to meet the evolving needs of your customers, ensuring their continued satisfaction.

4. Benchmarking against competitors:

Monitoring review trends not only helps you understand your own business but also provides an opportunity to benchmark against your competitors. By analyzing the reviews of your competitors, you can gain insights into their strengths and weaknesses, identify areas where you can differentiate yourself, and stay competitive in the market.

7.4.2 Effective Strategies for Monitoring Review Trends

Now that we understand the importance of monitoring review trends, let's explore some effective strategies to help you stay on top of the feedback you receive:

1. Set up review alerts:

Many online platforms, including Etsy, offer review alert features that notify you whenever a new review is posted. Take advantage of these alerts to stay informed in real-time and respond promptly to customer feedback.

2. Use review management tools:

Consider using review management tools that can aggregate reviews from multiple platforms and provide you with comprehensive analytics. These tools can help you track review trends, sentiment analysis, and customer satisfaction metrics, saving you time and effort in manual monitoring.

3. Categorize and analyze reviews:

Create a system for categorizing and analyzing reviews based on different criteria such as product, service, or specific concerns. This will allow you to identify patterns and trends more easily and make data-driven decisions to improve your business.

4. Pay attention to sentiment analysis:

In addition to reading individual reviews, pay attention to sentiment analysis tools that can automatically analyze the sentiment (positive, negative, or neutral) of reviews. This will give you a high-level overview of the overall sentiment towards your business and help you identify any shifts or trends.

5. Regularly review and update your strategies:

Review trends can change over time, so it's important to regularly review and update your monitoring strategies. Stay up to date with the latest tools and techniques for monitoring review trends and adapt your approach as needed to ensure you are capturing the most relevant insights.

7.4.3 Leveraging Review Trends for Business Growth

Monitoring and analyzing review trends is not just about identifying areas for improvement; it can also be a powerful tool for business growth. Here are a few ways you can leverage review trends to drive your business forward:

1. Highlight positive trends in marketing materials:

If you notice positive trends in your reviews, such as consistent praise for a particular product or service, leverage that feedback in your marketing materials. Highlighting these positive trends can help build trust and credibility with potential customers and encourage them to choose your business over competitors.

2. Incorporate customer feedback into product development:

Review trends can provide valuable insights into what customers love about your products and services and what they would like to see improved. Use this feedback to inform your product development process and make enhancements that align with customer preferences.

3. Train and motivate your team:

Share review trends with your team to keep them informed about customer feedback and motivate them to deliver exceptional customer experiences. Positive trends can serve as a morale booster, while negative trends can highlight areas where additional training or support may be needed.

4. Engage with customers based on trends:

If you notice recurring themes or concerns in reviews, proactively engage with customers to address those issues. This demonstrates your commitment to customer satisfaction and can help turn negative experiences into positive ones.

By monitoring and analyzing review trends, you can gain valuable insights into the sentiment of your customers, identify areas for improvement, and leverage positive feedback for business growth. Make it a priority to regularly review and analyze your reviews, and use the insights gained to continuously enhance your products, services, and customer experiences.

8 Handling Feedback and Continuous Improvement

8.1 The Value of Feedback for Business Growth

Feedback is an invaluable tool for business growth. It provides valuable insights into the customer experience, helps identify areas for improvement, and allows businesses to make informed decisions. In this section, we will explore the importance of feedback and how it can contribute to the success of your business.

8.1.1 Understanding the Importance of Feedback

Feedback is a powerful tool that allows businesses to understand their customers' needs, preferences, and expectations. It provides a direct line of communication between businesses and their customers, enabling them to gather valuable insights and make informed decisions.

One of the key benefits of feedback is that it helps businesses identify areas for improvement. By listening to their customers' feedback, businesses can identify pain points, address issues, and enhance their products or services. This continuous improvement process is crucial for staying competitive in today's fast-paced business environment.

Moreover, feedback plays a vital role in building customer loyalty and trust. When customers feel heard and valued, they are more likely to become repeat customers and advocates for your brand. By actively seeking and responding to feedback, businesses can foster strong relationships with their customers and create a positive brand image.

8.1.2 Creating a Feedback Loop with Customers

To harness the power of feedback, businesses need to establish a feedback loop with their customers. This involves actively seeking feedback, listening to customer concerns, and responding in a timely and meaningful manner.

There are several ways to collect feedback from customers. One common method is through online review platforms like Etsy, where customers can leave reviews and ratings. It is essential for businesses to monitor these platforms regularly and respond to both positive and negative reviews.

Another effective way to gather feedback is through surveys and questionnaires. By asking targeted questions, businesses can gain specific insights into customer satisfaction, product preferences, and areas for improvement. These surveys can be conducted through email, social media, or even in-person interactions.

Additionally, businesses can encourage customers to provide feedback through incentives such as discounts, loyalty points, or exclusive offers. This not only motivates customers to share their thoughts but also shows that their feedback is valued.

8.1.3 Implementing Changes Based on Feedback

Collecting feedback is only the first step. To truly benefit from feedback, businesses must take action and implement changes based on the insights gained. This demonstrates to customers that their feedback is being heard and acted upon.

When analyzing feedback, businesses should look for common themes or patterns. Are there specific issues that multiple customers are highlighting? Are there any recurring suggestions for improvement? By identifying these trends, businesses can prioritize their efforts and make targeted changes that will have the most significant impact.

It is important to involve relevant stakeholders, such as product managers, customer service representatives, and marketing teams, in the feedback analysis process. This ensures that different perspectives are considered and that the necessary resources are allocated to address the identified issues.

Once changes have been implemented, it is crucial to communicate these updates to customers. This can be done through email newsletters, social media posts, or even personalized messages to customers who provided feedback. By keeping customers informed, businesses can demonstrate their commitment to continuous improvement and maintain customer satisfaction.

8.1.4 Measuring the Impact of Feedback on Reviews

To gauge the effectiveness of feedback implementation, businesses should monitor and analyze review trends. By tracking changes in review ratings, sentiment, and customer feedback over time, businesses can assess the impact of their efforts.

Review analytics tools can provide valuable insights into review trends, allowing businesses to identify improvements in customer satisfaction and overall sentiment. These tools can also help identify any new challenges or areas for further improvement.

In addition to review analytics, businesses can also measure the impact of feedback on key performance indicators (KPIs) such as customer retention, sales, and brand reputation. By comparing these metrics before and after implementing feedback-driven changes, businesses can quantify the benefits of their efforts.

It is important to note that feedback is an ongoing process. As businesses evolve and customer expectations change, feedback should continue to be collected and acted upon. By embracing feedback as a valuable resource, businesses can drive continuous improvement, enhance customer satisfaction, and ultimately achieve long-term growth.

In the next section, we will explore how to create a feedback loop with customers and implement changes based on their feedback.

8.2 Creating a Feedback Loop with Customers

Creating a feedback loop with customers is an essential aspect of building a successful business. By actively seeking and listening to customer feedback, you can gain valuable insights into their experiences, identify areas for improvement, and ultimately enhance your products and services. In this section, we will explore the importance of creating a feedback loop with customers and provide practical strategies for effectively collecting and utilizing customer feedback.

8.2.1 The Importance of Customer Feedback

Customer feedback is a powerful tool that can help you understand your customers' needs, preferences, and pain points. It provides you with valuable insights into how your products or services are perceived and used, allowing you to make informed decisions about improvements and enhancements. Here are some key reasons why creating a feedback loop with customers is crucial:

1. **Identifying areas for improvement**: Customer feedback can highlight areas where your business may be falling short or where there is room for improvement. By actively seeking feedback, you can identify pain points and address them proactively, ensuring customer satisfaction and loyalty.
2. **Enhancing customer experience**: By listening to customer feedback, you can gain a deeper understanding of their expectations and preferences. This knowledge allows you to tailor your products, services, and overall customer experience to meet their needs, resulting in higher customer satisfaction and loyalty.
3. **Building customer trust and loyalty**: When customers see that their feedback is valued and acted upon, it builds trust and strengthens the relationship between your business and its customers. This, in turn, leads to increased customer loyalty and advocacy.
4. **Staying ahead of the competition**: By actively seeking and utilizing customer feedback, you can stay ahead of

the competition by continuously improving your offerings. This proactive approach demonstrates your commitment to meeting customer needs and sets you apart from competitors who may not prioritize customer feedback.

8.2.2 Strategies for Collecting Customer Feedback

To create an effective feedback loop with customers, you need to implement strategies for collecting feedback consistently and efficiently. Here are some strategies you can use:

1. **Surveys and questionnaires**: Create surveys or questionnaires that allow customers to provide feedback on their experiences. Keep the surveys concise and focused on specific aspects of your business to encourage higher response rates.
2. **In-person feedback**: If you have a physical store or interact with customers face-to-face, encourage them to provide feedback directly. This can be done through comment cards, suggestion boxes, or even casual conversations.
3. **Online reviews and ratings**: Monitor and analyze online reviews and ratings on platforms like Etsy, social media, and review websites. These platforms provide a wealth of customer feedback that can help you identify trends and areas for improvement.
4. **Customer feedback forms**: Include a feedback form on your website or in your email communications. Make it easy for customers to provide feedback by keeping the form simple and straightforward.
5. **Social media listening**: Monitor social media platforms for mentions of your business or products. Engage with customers who leave feedback or comments, and use this opportunity to gather additional insights.
6. **Focus groups and user testing**: Organize focus groups or conduct user testing sessions to gather more in-depth feedback from a select group of customers. This can provide valuable insights into specific aspects of your business or new product ideas.

8.2.3 Utilizing Customer Feedback

Collecting customer feedback is only the first step; the real value lies in how you utilize that feedback to drive improvements and enhance your business. Here are some strategies for effectively utilizing customer feedback:

1. **Analyze and categorize feedback**: Review and categorize the feedback you receive to identify common themes or issues. This will help you prioritize areas for improvement and develop targeted solutions.
2. **Act promptly**: Address customer feedback promptly and take immediate action where necessary. This demonstrates your commitment to customer satisfaction and shows that their feedback is valued.
3. **Communicate changes and improvements**: When you make changes or improvements based on customer feedback, communicate these updates to your customers. This not only shows that you are actively listening but also keeps customers informed and engaged.
4. **Track and measure impact**: Monitor the impact of changes implemented based on customer feedback. Use metrics such as customer satisfaction scores, repeat purchases, or positive reviews to measure the effectiveness of your improvements.
5. **Reward and recognize customers**: Show appreciation for customers who provide feedback by offering incentives or rewards. This encourages ongoing participation in your feedback loop and strengthens the customer-business relationship.
6. **Continuously iterate and improve**: Creating a feedback loop is an ongoing process. Regularly review and

refine your feedback collection strategies, and use customer feedback to drive continuous improvement in your products, services, and overall customer experience.

By actively creating a feedback loop with your customers, you can harness the power of their insights to drive continuous improvement and enhance your business. Remember, customer feedback is a valuable resource that can help you build trust, loyalty, and credibility while staying ahead of the competition. Embrace feedback as an opportunity for growth and use it to shape a stellar customer experience.

8.3 Implementing Changes Based on Feedback

Receiving feedback from customers is an invaluable resource for any business. It provides insights into what is working well and areas that need improvement. In order to truly benefit from feedback, it is important to not only listen to what customers are saying but also take action to implement changes based on their suggestions. This chapter will guide you through the process of implementing changes based on feedback, ensuring that you are continuously improving your products and services.

8.3.1 Analyzing Feedback

Before implementing any changes, it is crucial to thoroughly analyze the feedback you receive. This involves categorizing the feedback into different themes or topics, identifying common patterns, and prioritizing the areas that require immediate attention. By analyzing feedback, you can gain a deeper understanding of your customers' needs and expectations.

One effective way to analyze feedback is by using sentiment analysis tools. These tools can help you determine the overall sentiment of the feedback, whether it is positive, negative, or neutral. Additionally, you can manually review each piece of feedback to extract valuable insights and identify specific areas for improvement.

8.3.2 Prioritizing Changes

Once you have analyzed the feedback, it is important to prioritize the changes that need to be implemented. Not all feedback will require immediate action, so it is essential to focus on the areas that will have the greatest impact on your customers' experience.

Consider the frequency and severity of the feedback when prioritizing changes. If multiple customers have raised the same issue, it is a clear indication that it needs to be addressed promptly. Similarly, if the feedback highlights a critical flaw in your product or service, it should be given high priority.

8.3.3 Developing an Action Plan

After prioritizing the changes, it is time to develop an action plan. This plan should outline the specific steps that need to be taken to address the feedback and improve your products or services. It is important to be clear and specific in your action plan, ensuring that everyone involved understands their roles and responsibilities.

Consider involving relevant stakeholders, such as your product development team or customer service representatives, in the action planning process. Their expertise and insights can contribute to the effectiveness of the changes you implement.

8.3.4 Communicating Changes to Customers

Once you have implemented the necessary changes, it is important to communicate them to your customers. This can be done through various channels, such as email newsletters, social media posts, or updates on your website. By informing your customers about the changes you have made, you demonstrate your commitment to their satisfaction and show that you value their feedback.

When communicating changes, be transparent and honest about the feedback you received and the actions you have taken. This helps build trust and credibility with your customers, showing them that their feedback is taken seriously and acted upon.

8.3.5 Monitoring the Impact of Changes

Implementing changes based on feedback is not the end of the process. It is crucial to monitor the impact of these changes to ensure they are effective and achieving the desired results. This can be done by tracking key performance indicators (KPIs) related to customer satisfaction, such as review ratings, customer retention rates, or repeat purchases.

Regularly review and analyze the data to assess the impact of the changes. If the desired results are not being achieved, it may be necessary to revisit the action plan and make further adjustments. Continuous monitoring and evaluation allow you to fine-tune your approach and ensure that the changes you implement are truly making a positive difference.

8.3.6 Involving Customers in the Process

In addition to implementing changes based on feedback, involving customers in the process can further enhance their experience and satisfaction. Consider seeking input from customers through surveys, focus groups, or beta testing programs. By involving them in the decision-making process, you not only make them feel valued but also gain valuable insights and ideas for improvement.

Furthermore, keep an open line of communication with your customers and encourage them to provide ongoing feedback. This can be done through various channels, such as email, social media, or dedicated feedback forms on your website. By actively seeking feedback, you create a culture of continuous improvement and ensure that your customers' voices are heard.

Implementing changes based on feedback is a continuous and iterative process. By analyzing feedback, prioritizing changes, developing an action plan, communicating changes to customers, monitoring the impact, and involving customers in the process, you can continuously improve your products and services to meet and exceed customer expectations. Remember, feedback is a valuable resource that can drive your business growth and success. Embrace it, learn from it, and use it to continuously evolve and thrive.

8.4 Measuring the Impact of Feedback on Reviews

As a business owner or manager, it is crucial to understand the impact of feedback on your reviews. Feedback plays a significant role in shaping the perception of your business and can greatly influence the overall rating and reputation of your products or services. In this section, we will explore the importance of measuring the impact of feedback on reviews and how you can effectively analyze and utilize this information to improve your business.

8.4.1 Understanding the Importance of Measuring Feedback

Measuring the impact of feedback on reviews is essential for several reasons. Firstly, it allows you to gauge the overall satisfaction level of your customers and identify areas for improvement. By analyzing the feedback received, you can gain valuable insights into what aspects of your business are working well and what areas need attention.

Secondly, measuring feedback helps you track the effectiveness of any changes or improvements you have implemented based on previous feedback. It allows you to assess whether these changes have had a positive impact on customer satisfaction and subsequently on your reviews.

Lastly, measuring feedback provides you with a benchmark to compare your performance against competitors. By understanding how your business is perceived in comparison to others in your industry, you can identify opportunities for differentiation and improvement.

8.4.2 Collecting and Analyzing Feedback

To measure the impact of feedback on reviews, you need to have a systematic approach to collecting and analyzing customer feedback. Here are some steps you can take:

1. **Implement a feedback collection system:** Set up a mechanism to collect feedback from your customers. This can be through surveys, feedback forms on your website, or even through direct communication channels such as email or phone calls. Make it easy for customers to provide feedback and encourage them to do so.
2. **Categorize and organize feedback:** Once you start receiving feedback, categorize it based on different aspects of your business such as product quality, customer service, or shipping experience. This will help you identify patterns and trends in the feedback.
3. **Analyze feedback for common themes:** Look for common themes or issues that are consistently mentioned in the feedback. These could be positive aspects that customers appreciate or areas where improvements are needed.
4. **Quantify feedback:** Assign a numerical value or rating to each feedback item to quantify the impact. This will help you track changes over time and measure the overall impact on your reviews.
5. **Compare feedback with reviews:** Analyze how the feedback you receive aligns with the reviews you receive. Look for correlations between positive feedback and positive reviews, as well as negative feedback and negative reviews. This will help you understand the direct impact of feedback on your reviews.

8.4.3 Utilizing Feedback to Improve Reviews

Once you have measured the impact of feedback on your reviews, it is essential to utilize this information effectively to improve your business. Here are some strategies you can implement:

1. **Address common issues:** Use the feedback you receive to identify common issues or concerns raised by customers. Take proactive steps to address these issues and make improvements where necessary. By resolving these issues, you can prevent negative reviews and improve overall customer satisfaction.
2. **Implement changes based on feedback:** If you consistently receive feedback regarding a specific aspect of your business that needs improvement, take action to implement changes. This could involve revising your product or service offerings, improving customer service processes, or enhancing your website or online presence.
3. **Communicate improvements to customers:** Once you have made changes based on feedback, communicate

these improvements to your customers. This can be done through email newsletters, social media posts, or updates on your website. By sharing the changes you have made, you demonstrate your commitment to customer satisfaction and encourage positive reviews.

4. **Monitor the impact of changes:** Continuously monitor the impact of the changes you have implemented based on feedback. Track the number and sentiment of reviews before and after the changes to assess their effectiveness. This will help you understand whether the changes have had a positive impact on your reviews and overall customer satisfaction.

8.4.4 Tracking Review Trends

In addition to measuring the impact of feedback on reviews, it is important to track review trends over time. This will help you identify any patterns or changes in customer sentiment and make informed decisions to improve your business. Here are some ways to track review trends:

1. **Monitor review platforms:** Regularly check review platforms such as Etsy, Google, or Yelp to see the latest reviews of your business. Pay attention to the overall rating, as well as the content of the reviews.

2. **Use review tracking tools:** Utilize review tracking tools that can aggregate reviews from multiple platforms and provide you with insights and analytics. These tools can help you identify trends, track sentiment, and measure the impact of feedback on your reviews.

3. **Set up alerts:** Set up alerts or notifications for new reviews so that you can respond promptly and address any concerns raised by customers. This will show your commitment to customer satisfaction and can help mitigate the impact of negative reviews.

4. **Analyze review data:** Regularly analyze the review data you collect to identify any trends or patterns. Look for changes in sentiment, common themes, or areas where improvements are needed. This analysis will provide you with valuable insights to guide your business decisions and improve your reviews.

By measuring the impact of feedback on reviews and tracking review trends, you can gain valuable insights into the satisfaction level of your customers and make informed decisions to improve your business. Remember, reviews are a powerful tool for building trust and credibility, and by effectively utilizing feedback, you can enhance your reputation and drive business success.